KU-487-073

The Observer's Pocket Series
MUSIC

D1239930

The Observer Books

A POCKET REFERENCE SERIES COVERING A WIDE RANGE OF SUBJECTS

Natural History

BIRDS
BIRDS' EGGS
BUTTERFLIES
LARGER MOTHS
COMMON INSECTS
WILD ANIMALS
ZOO ANIMALS
WILD FLOWERS
GARDEN FLOWERS
FLOWERING TREES
   AND SHRUBS
HOUSE PLANTS
CACTI
TREES
GRASSES
FERNS
COMMON FUNGI
LICHENS
POND LIFE
FRESHWATER FISHES
SEA FISHES
SEA AND SEASHORE
GEOLOGY
ASTRONOMY
WEATHER
CATS
DOGS
HORSES AND PONIES

Transport

AIRCRAFT
AUTOMOBILES
COMMERCIAL VEHICLES
SHIPS
MANNED SPACEFLIGHT
UNMANNED SPACEFLIGHT
MOTOR SPORT
STEAM LOCOMOTIVES

The Arts etc

ARCHITECTURE
CATHEDRALS
CHURCHES
HERALDRY
FLAGS
PAINTING
MODERN ART
SCULPTURE
FURNITURE
POTTERY AND PORCELAIN
MUSIC
POSTAGE STAMPS
EUROPEAN COSTUME
AWARDS AND MEDALS

Sport

ASSOCIATION FOOTBALL
CRICKET

Cities

LONDON

The Observer's Book of
MUSIC

By
FREDA DINN
G.R.C.M., A.R.C.M., A.T.C.L.

Illustrated by
PAUL SHARP
A.R.C.A., A.T.D.

Sections on:
Sound; musical instruments;
concert programme terms; composers.
With numerous illustrations
many of which are in colour.

FREDERICK WARNE & CO LTD
FREDERICK WARNE & CO INC
LONDON: NEW YORK

Copyright in all countries
signatory to the Berne Convention

FREDERICK WARNE & CO. LTD.
LONDON, ENGLAND
1953

Revised Edn. 1959
Seventh reprint 1975

ISBN 0 7232 0058 0

Printed in Great Britain

INTRODUCTION

FOR MOST of us who have ' ears to hear ', listening to music is a source of delight. Greater knowledge can enrich our enjoyment in no small measure, but this knowledge need not necessarily be technical, although the ability to follow music from the printed page may often help us to enjoy it more.

In this book, music is considered from the particular angle of the observer or listener searching for the answers to some of his many questions, and it is hoped that because of this, it may find its way into the pocket of the music-lover for consultation during and after concerts. It is hoped, too, that radio listeners will find equal pleasure in ' dipping ' into these pages.

The reader will find detailed descriptions of instruments and how they work, meanings of unfamiliar words on the programme or concert advertisement, and notes on the lives and works of composers, while the first chapter, on Sound, has its own special interest.

A few elementary musical terms have been used, and readers are probably familiar with them, but for those who wish to consult it, an Appendix explaining some terms used within the text, together with a chart of the pianoforte keyboard, is to be found at the end of the book.

Our thanks are due to Mr. Will Chanot for making possible some of the illustrations in the

5

chapter on strings; to Messrs. Boosey and
Hawkes for the loan of photographs of wind
instruments, and to Mr. L. F. Lamerton, Ph.D.,
for reading the script and for help with the chapter
on sound.

FREDA DINN
PAUL SHARP

CONTENTS

An Arrangemen

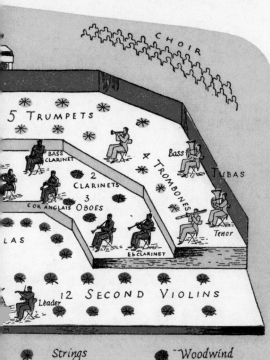

CHOIR

5 TRUMPETS

BASS CLARINET

2 CLARINETS

3

COR ANGLAIS OBOES

Bass

4 TROMBONES

TUBAS

Tenor

Eb CLARINET

LAS

12 SECOND VIOLINS

Leader

* Strings

* Brass

● Woodwind

✳ Percussion

f the Orchestra

PART ONE

Sound

CHAPTER I

SOUND AND HOW WE HEAR IT

WE CAN enjoy music and at the same time have very little knowledge of its production. For most of us, however, some knowledge of the how and why of the production of musical sounds will not only have an interest for its own sake, but will also help to increase our enjoyment of music.

Let us imagine we are in a concert-hall listening to an orchestra. What are the various steps in the process which begins with the effort expended by each player on his instrument and ends with our enjoyment of listening to the resultant sounds ? The final question, why we should feel a sense of enjoyment in certain combinations of sounds, is a philosophical one, and cannot concern us here. We can, however, say something about the mechanism of the sensation of sound.

We hear sound when our ear-drums are made to vibrate under the influence of disturbances in the air around us. These disturbances in the air will consist of a flow of alternate compressions and rarefactions of the air itself. A note of given pitch will be heard when the series of compressions and rarefactions follow each other in regular succession. When the succession of these "vibrations" in the air has no regularity, a "noise" and not a "note" will be heard.

The speed at which sound travels is at the rate of about 1,100 feet per second. If we are in a very large hall, at the back, watching an orchestra as well as listening to it, it is likely that we shall hear the sounds from the orchestra a moment or two after they appear to have been produced. Sound-waves can be reflected from hard surfaces, and their behaviour is not unlike that of light-waves. If we are in a hall, we shall find that there will be more resonance from music performed in it when it is almost empty, than when it is full of people, because we shall hear not only the sound coming direct from the instruments, but also the reflections from the hard surfaces of walls and floor and empty seats. Such resonance is particularly noticeable in a cathedral or lofty church, and in no small measure adds to the "ethereal" quality of the singing of the choir. In a concert hall the results can be much less pleasing, and there may be so much resonance that the music sounds blurred. Through advancement in the knowledge of acoustics, resonance can be controlled, as it has been, for example, in the construction of the Royal Festival Hall, London.

Sound waves vary in two ways, in loudness or softness, and in pitch. The greater the agitation in the air, the louder the sound; the amount of agitation is called the amplitude, and the degree of loudness is therefore determined by the degree of amplitude. The pitch of any note depends on the number of vibrations per second which reach the ear-drum: the more vibrations per second (the higher the frequency), the higher the

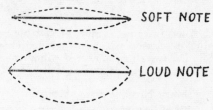

Soft and Loud Sound Waves

pitch of the note; the less vibrations per second (the lower the frequency), the lower the pitch of the note. The first note we are likely to hear coming from the whole orchestra will be the tuning note, A, given by the oboe and "tuned-to" by all the instruments of the orchestra, except, of course, some of the percussion. Instruments tuning to the pitch A: will be producing a note having 440 vibrations per second. Some of the large instruments whose pitch-range is lower will tune to the A an octave below the oboe's A, which has 220 vibrations per second. It is likely that the piccolo, the smallest instrument, and therefore the highest-pitched instrument of the orchestra, will sound the A an octave above that of the oboe : that note will have 880 vibrations per second.

Here are the three As with their frequencies :

Each A has twice the number of vibrations per second of the A an octave below it ; and in fact, any note has twice the number of vibrations per second of the note an octave below it.

MAIN NOTES AND OVERTONES

The musical instrument, whatever its shape or size, is a device for setting the air into regular vibrations. It produces notes which are complex—that is, in addition to the main note which we hear, and can name, there are other tones of higher frequency which vibrate within the note we consciously hear. Any note, therefore, which we hear consists of the lowest tone, and a number of other tones, higher in pitch, which blend with it. The relative intensities of the various overtones fix the " quality " or timbre of a note and they are responsible for the difference in tone quality, between, for instance, an oboe, a clarinet, a flute and a violin. The overtones conform to a definite pattern in relation to one another. The complete pattern is known as the harmonic series. With certain exceptions the possible overtones have frequencies which are in the ratio of 2, 3, 4, 5, 6, etc., to the fundamental.

In musical notation the notes of the harmonic series are known as the *fundamental, the octave,* the *twelfth,* etc. Taking C as the fundamental the harmonic series is as follows:

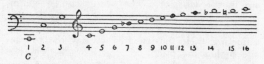

The notes in black are slightly flatter than those found on a keyboard.

We may now begin to answer a question that will certainly occur to us while studying the orchestra: Why have the instruments such different shapes? And what are the general principles underlying the curious appearance of some of the instruments?

VIBRATORS AND RESONATORS

All musical instruments are made up of two parts: a *vibrator*, which the performer sets into motion, and a *resonator*, which serves to enhance the sound produced by the vibrator, and to send the sound-waves into the air. In the violin family the string is the vibrator, and the body of the violin, with its enclosed air, is the resonator. With a trumpet, the player's lips are the vibrator, and the air inside the tube of the trumpet is the resonator.

It is, however, necessary to make a distinction between the various classes of instruments.

Firstly, there is the class of instrument in which the resonator will enhance notes over a range of pitch and where the pitch of the note produced is determined by the rate of vibration actually set up in the vibrator. The string family—violin, viola, violoncello and double bass—are in this class. After the strings have been tuned by adjusting their tension (the greater the tension the higher the pitch), the pitch of the notes is determined by the position of the player's fingers on the strings—the shorter the vibrating portion of the string, the higher the pitch of the note. The actual sound produced from a vibrating string would not be resonant enough to be of any musical value, so the vibrations produced from the string are amplified and endowed with that particular tone-quality which is associated with instruments of the string family by the vibrations of the belly and back of the instrument and the resounding cavity of air contained in its body. These vibrations communicate with the atmosphere through the holes in the belly of the instrument. Furthermore, the individual tone-qualities of the violin, the viola, the violoncello and double-bass are determined by these resonators.

The same principle of resonance is applied to keyboard instruments having strings, and to the harp. The pitch is determined by the particular string set in vibration by being either struck, as in the pianoforte, or plucked, as in the harp. The resonance is provided by a thin pine-wood sounding-board.

The kettle-drum consists also of a vibrator, the stretched skin set in vibration by the player's stick, and a resonator, the air contained in the copper shell of the instrument.

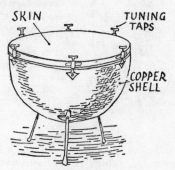

The Kettle-drum

Secondly, there is the class of instruments in which the resonator will enhance only certain notes, and once the vibrator has been set in motion, its rate of vibration will be determined by the resonator itself. The wood-wind and brass-wind instruments are in this class. When, for instance, a player blows across the mouth-hole of a flute, which is a wood-wind instrument open at both ends, a stream of air from a narrow slit moves against the column of stagnant air, and forms little eddies. The player blows against the sharp edge of the mouth-hole to coerce these eddies into order and to produce what is known as an "edge-tone". The stagnant air inside the flute is set in motion by the vibration of the edge-tone, and a note sounds, the pitch being determined by the length of the enclosed air-column.

If a pipe is closed at one end, as is the case with the clarinet, the sounds made will be different, since the vibrations within the pipe will differ. The column of air travelling down the pipe will be reflected at the closed end, and it will again be reflected on reaching the open end, owing to the elasticity of the surrounding air, and a series of waves will travel up and down the pipe. The pitch of the note will depend on the time taken for a compression to travel down the pipe and back again to the open end, that is, on the length of the pipe. These eddies in their travelling agitate the air in varying degrees. A point of greatest agitation is known as an antinode, and a point of least agitation is known as a node. At the "stopped" or closed end of a pipe there is always a node, and at the open end—at the bell of an instrument, for instance—there is always an antinode.

A column of air in an open pipe can be made to vibrate to the sub-divisions shown in the diagram

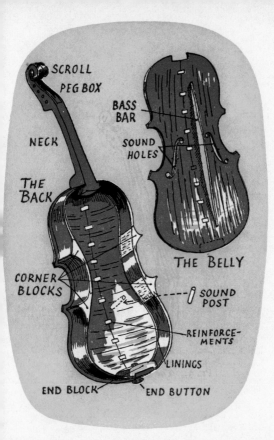

SCROLL
PEG BOX
BASS BAR
NECK
SOUND HOLES
THE BACK
THE BELLY
CORNER BLOCKS
SOUND POST
REINFORCEMENTS
LININGS
END BLOCK
END BUTTON

PL. 2.   *An Opened Violin* (p. 25)

PL. 3.   *The Treble Viol* (p. 35)

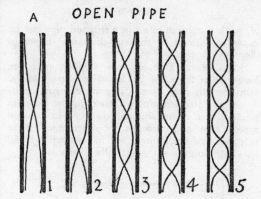

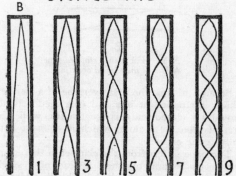

Sub-divisions of a Column of Air in A an Open Pipe,
B a Stopped Pipe

A, while a column of air in a stopped pipe can be made to vibrate in the sub-divisions shown in diagram *B*.

Sound-waves formed in a stopped pipe are longer than those formed in an open pipe of the same length and bore. The fundamental produced in a stopped pipe will therefore be lower in pitch than the fundamental produced in an open pipe. The sub-divisions or harmonics in a stopped pipe are limited, but in an open pipe all the harmonics are theoretically available.

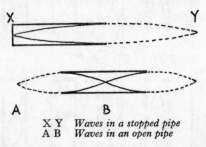

X Y   *Waves in a stopped pipe*
A B   *Waves in an open pipe*

Because of this, the first overtone of a clarinet, which is stopped at one end (the reed actually provides a closed end), is the twelfth, while the first overtone of a flute, which is open at both ends, is the octave.

The oboe differs from the clarinet in that it has two reeds beating together, instead of a single reed beating against a rigid " table ". Also its tube is conical, instead of being cylindrical. The note produced is governed by the conical column of air. By mathematical calculation, beyond the scope of this book, it can be shown that the harmonics of a conical column, closed at one end and open at the other, are similar to those of a cylindrical column open at both ends. The full harmonic series is available. The complex note of the oboe has a " reedy " tone, because the whole series of harmonics is contained in it, with some of them having a greater intensity than the fundamental.

The tone of the clarinet has its particular quality because only the odd-numbered notes of the harmonic series are present.

The characteristic thinness of the tone of the flute was brought about by Theobald Boehm (1793 or 1794 to 1881) of Munich (see page 67), who gave the flute its present-day form and appearance. It has already been stated that the flute has a cylindrical tube. In the Boehm flute there is, near the mouth-piece, a steady contraction of the bore towards the mouth-piece which causes the overtones to deviate from the harmonic series 2, 3, 4, etc., and because of this, they are not resonant, and are called " in-harmonic ". In this type of flute, therefore, the tone consists of little else than the fundamental.

In brass instruments the player's lips function in the same way as the double reed of an oboe. The player produces the note he wants by tightening his lips to get the higher notes, and holding them loose for the lower notes, since his lips must vibrate at the same frequency as the note of the column of air. If the mouth-piece is cup-shaped, the higher harmonics are formed, and the resultant tone is brilliant. If the mouth-piece is funnel-shaped, as on the horn, the tone will be more mellow, as the higher harmonics are not present.

If we want lower notes, we must have larger resonators ; if we want higher notes, we must have smaller resonators. It is for this reason that there are four different sizes of instruments in the string family : violin, viola, violoncello, double-bass. Some of the brass instruments are many feet long, and obviously, if they were straight it would be impossible for the player to hold them, let alone carry them ! It is for this reason, therefore, that brass instruments have such curious shapes. Of the wood-wind family, the bassoon is the largest instrument, and its long tube is bent in such a way that it somewhat resembles a bundle of sticks—hence its Italian name, " fagotto ".

As the stringed instruments in an orchestra do not individually possess the same tone-power as the other instruments, there are always more of them, and they are always placed nearest to the audience. As the sound produced radiates from the sound-holes in the bellies of stringed instru-ments, the orchestra is so arranged that as many string-players as possible have their instruments facing the audience.

The how and the why of the production of musical sounds have now been briefly described : more detail will be found later in this book, when each instrument is described. But what about the orchestral conductor? What does he really do? Each player in an orchestra is chiefly concerned with playing the music put before him to the best of his ability. The conductor is responsible for welding together all the separate parts into one complete whole, and he should be familiar with all the peculiarities, possibilities and shortcomings of the instruments in his orchestra, so that he can get the best possible results from his players. A great deal of this work is done during rehearsals. At a performance the conductor should not only direct his players, but he should also inspire them so that we as listeners might fully enjoy the realisation of the composer's vision.

PART TWO

Instruments of Today and Yesterday

CHAPTER II

STRINGED INSTRUMENTS: BOWED, PLUCKED, HIT

BOWED INSTRUMENTS

THE STRING FAMILY OF TODAY

A Member of Louis XIV's Band

Nowadays, when we refer to the *strings*, we have in mind the violin family, consisting of four members—namely, the violin, the viola, the violoncello and the contra- or double-bass. These have many similar characteristics, but one of the chief differences is their size, ranging from the violin (the smallest), playing the highest notes, to the double-bass (the largest), playing the lowest notes. On all these instruments the strings are set in vibration with a bow, but sometimes the strings are plucked with the fingers. As the quantity of tone is not as great from stringed instruments as from wind instruments, many more string players than wind players are required in an orchestra. In a large symphony orchestra there might be as many as eighteen first violins, sixteen second violins, twelve violoncelli, and eight double-basses.

The shape of the violin, as we know it today, emerged during the middle of the 16th century, in Italy, having been gradually evolved from the rebec, a small bowed instrument of medieval times. The name *violin* was applied to all the members of this family, and not to the smallest one only. Louis XIV had a band of " Twenty-four Violins " at his Court, and Charles II, on his return in 1660, set up a similar band in England. From this time the violin as such gained prestige in England, and the popularity of the viol gradually waned.

The members of the violin family have many similar features which are shown in the diagrams ; their individual characteristics will be found later in the description and illustration of each instrument.

The Production of the Sound

When the strings are set in vibration, the sound-waves travel through the bridge and sound-post to the hollow body of the instrument which acts

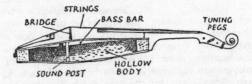

as a resonator, enhancing and amplifying the sound-waves ; thus changed, they flow out through the sound holes.

The strings are tuned by turning the pegs—the

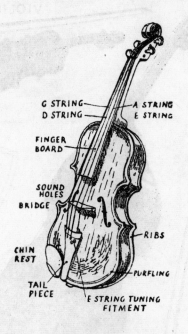

G STRING
D STRING
A STRING
E STRING
FINGER
BOARD
SOUND
HOLES
BRIDGE
RIBS
CHIN
REST
PURFLING
TAIL
PIECE
E STRING TUNING
FITMENT

PL. 4. *Front View of a Violin* (p. 28)

VIOLIN

The

DOUBLE
BASS

PL. 5.

VIOLA

Violin Family

1 foot

CELLO

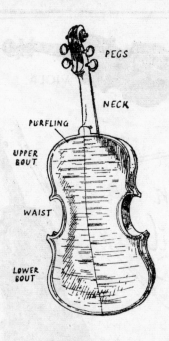

PL. 6.   *Back View of a Violin* (p. 28)

greater the tension, or pull, on the string, the higher the pitch. The strings are said to be "open" when they are sounded without any fingers placed upon them. Other notes are obtained by "stopping" the strings with the fingers of the left hand (pressing the strings to the finger-board, thus shortening their vibrating portion)—the shorter the string, the higher the pitch for the same tension. *Harmonics* can be produced by touching the strings very lightly with the fingers (instead of "stopping") at certain special places; for example, if a string is touched at half its length, the octave will be found; at a third of its length from either the bridge or the nut, the twelfth above will be found —and so on:

Materials Used (Pl. 2)

Most strings are made of prepared sheep-gut, cut in strips, and then tightly twisted. The lower strings on all the instruments are covered in fine metal wire—silver, copper or aluminium— in order to increase their resonance without adding to their length.

The table (or belly), bass bar, sound post, blocks and linings are made of pine, the back, ribs, neck and bridge are of sycamore, and the finger-board, tail-piece and nut of ebony, and the pegs are usually of rosewood.

To prevent the wood splitting across the body of the instrument after much use, and incidentally to enhance its appearance, a small groove is made near the edges of the belly and the back, into which three strips of lime-wood are inlaid (one is left light in colour, and the other two are stained black). This is known as *purfling*. Although a violin looks so delicate, it is carefully strengthened and reinforced inside by means of many pieces of wood of various sizes. The body and neck are covered with many coats of varnish to preserve the wood and to improve the tone and appearance.

The Mute

The tone can be given a nasal quality for a special effect by clamping a mute on the bridge.

The mute can be made of metal or ebony, or any suitable hard substance.

The Bow

By means of the bow, the sound of the vibrating string can be sustained as in singing, and while it is sustained it can be varied in intensity by the skilled player.

26

The bow consists of a *stick*, which must be strong, yet flexible (Pernambuco wood and snakewood are both good—they both come from South America), and the *hair* (horse's hair—from the tail), which is bleached for violin, viola and violoncello bows and left black for double-bass bows. By means of a screw the hair can be stretched for performance and slackened when not in use, to save the strain on the stick and the hair. When magnified, the hair shows "thorns", as on a rose-briar, which, with the aid of powdered resin, grip the string, causing it to vibrate when the bow is drawn across parallel to the bridge. The violin bow has over a hundred and fifty hairs.

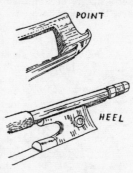

The production and variation of tone are governed mainly by the following three factors: the position of the bow on the string (its distance from the bridge); the pressure exerted on it; and the speed with which it travels over the string.

The bow only acquired its present shape towards the end of the 18th century, when a more sprightly style of bowing was required. Its shape and balance were changed (compare it with the viol bow), and its strength was transferred from the point to the heel. Today, some violinists of repute are using the older type of bow for a truer performance of violin works composed before the new bow came into use.

The Violin (Pl. 4, 5, 6)

As the violin was always played with one end under the chin, its length was determined by the

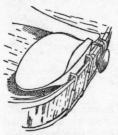

average length of the player's arm, which must be comfortably bent (as shown in Pl. 9).

A chin-rest is fixed to the instrument, and many players use a pad between the shoulder and the violin, so that it can be comfortably held without the aid of the left hand, which must be free to move.

The lowest note is G below middle C, and it is possible for a skilled player to get as many notes as there are to the top of the piano keyboard. The four strings are tuned in perfect fifths—A is always tuned first:

When the terms *first violin* and *second violin* are used, they are a reference to the parts played, comparable with the first and second soprano voices in a choir: the instruments themselves are identical. In an orchestra the first violins are always on the left of the conductor, so that the

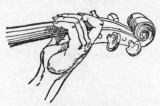

*Position of the Left Hand
on the Violin and Viola*

tone from them is directed towards the audience. The leader of the first violins is an important person, who is known also as the leader of the orchestra, and he is sometimes called upon to conduct. The second violins will be found either on the right of the conductor or on the left of the first violins. In chamber music (music for several instruments, with one player to each part) the first violin always leads.

The Viola

The viola is played in the same way as the violin, but, as it plays at a lower pitch, it has to be bigger, the strings are thicker and the bow is heavier. A great deal of its music is written in the alto clef (Middle C being the middle of the five lines), in order to avoid so many leger lines, or the constant changing of treble and bass clefs.

The Viola

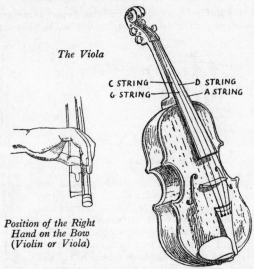

*Position of the Right
Hand on the Bow
(Violin or Viola)*

It is no more difficult to read in this clef than in the treble or bass, once it is learnt (see pages 184–5).

Middle C

Bass, Alto, and Treble Clefs

The normal pitch range is from C below middle C, extending over about three octaves :

30

In an orchestra the viola-players are usually seated in front of the conductor, and the viola tone can be distinguished from that of the violins because it is often more mellow.

Until recent times the viola was considered the "Cinderella" of the family, and was ignored as a solo instrument.

The Violoncello ('cello) (Pl. 7)

The 'cello is too large to be played under the chin, so it is placed between the knees and is supported by an adjustable pin. The bow is shorter and heavier than a viola bow, and the strings are thicker and longer.

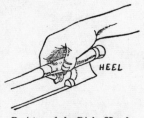

HEEL

Position of the Right Hand on the Bow

The lowest note obtainable is C two octaves below middle C, and it has an extensive pitch-range above this, which is especially useful for solo passages. The player has to be familiar with three clefs : the bass, the tenor and the treble :

Bass, Tenor, and Treble Clefs

The open strings are :

Position of the Left Hand on the Body of the 'Cello

When the left hand has to travel above the body of the 'cello in the " higher positions ", the thumb (as well as the fingers) is used for stopping the strings.

The 'cello tone can be bright and clear, and can have a " cutting " quality in the higher notes.

The Double-bass (often called the *Contra-bass*, or *bass* for short) (Pl. 8)

This is a hybrid between the old violone and the violin family. It retains the characteristics of the viol in shape, tuning in fourths and method of bowing. It has a stronger body, however, and sometimes three strings have been used, but now four are usually used.

The double-bass is known as a transposing instrument because the notes played are different from those written (actually an octave lower).

The open strings are :

32

PL. 7. *Piatti (1822–1901), an Italian 'cellist.*
('Cello—p. 31)

PL. 8.   *Bottesini* (1821–89), *a famous Double-bass
player, playing on the Three-stringed Bass.
(Double-bass—p. 32)*

Some Signs and Terms used in Modern String Music

arco : with the bow.

∏ (*down bow*) : in the direction of heel to point.

∨ (*up bow*) : in the direction of point to heel.

pizzicato : pluck the strings.

+ : pluck with the fingers of the left hand.

⌒ : a bowing mark (phrase slur), indicating that all notes embraced by it are to be played with the bow travelling in the same direction.

O : open string or harmonic.

Changing position : moving the left hand up or down the neck of the instrument.

vibrato : the " wobble " in a sound, made by swiftly rolling the finger tip on the stopped string.

double ⎰ *stopping* : sounding more than one string
triple ⎱ at a time.

spiccato : light, springy bowing.

col legno (rare) : play with the stick of the bow.

con sordino : with the mute.

senza sordino : without the mute.

*　　*　　*　　*　　*

EARLY VIOLINS

The Rebec. The rebec came from the East, and was in use throughout western Europe during

The Rebec

the Middle Ages. It was the *small fiddle* in England, the *geige* in Germany and the *gigue* in France. It is believed that the English Jig—the dance—was so named from the instrument which provided the tune.

It is made from one piece of shaped wood, part of which is hollowed out and then covered in with a flat board of pine-wood to make

a resonator (like the body of the violin). It has three gut-strings, tuned A D G (like the violin), and its tone is nasal and harsh in quality.

The Kit or Pocket Violin (Fr. *Pochette*). This was used by French dandies and dancing-masters during the 17th century, and it continued to be used by dancing-masters until the middle of the 19th century. It

A Dancing-Master with his Kit

34

was so called because it could be carried, together with its small, dainty bow, in the coat pocket.

THE VIOLS (Pl. 16)

There was a rudimentary form of viol as early as the 11th century. During the 15th century the viol was improved in Italy, where it acquired its present form and its six strings. It became popular for the performance of Fancies and Consorts. (See pages 126 and 128.)

Owing to the depth of the sides of the viol and the flatness of its back, the sound is soft, reedy and penetrating.

In England it acquired the name *Viol*: in Italy *Viola de Gamba* (" leg-viol ") because it is held between the legs. There are three usual sizes: the *Treble* (Pl. 3), tuned thus:

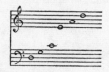

the *Bass*, tuned an octave lower, and the *Tenor* or *Mean*, a fourth of fifth below the Treble. A chest of viols, for home use, could include six viols, two of each size.

Towards the end of the 17th century the *Division Viol*—a slightly smaller form of bass viol—became popular for the performance of Divisions variations on a ground bass (a simple recurring melody). At this time the smaller viols

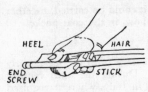

*Position of the Right Hand on
the Bow of the Treble Viol*

were ousted out by the violins in this country, but the bass viol survived for nearly another hundred years.

Viols are now being revived both here and abroad, and they can be heard quite frequently.

The Violone, or double-bass viol, was a large instrument playing an octave lower than the bass viol, and was common in Italy and Germany (see Double-bass, page 32).

It will be noticed that the viol bow is different in shape from the modern bow. The strongest part is at the point, whereas in the modern bow it

is at the heel. There is no ferrule, and the hair can be pushed away from the stick by the fingers and made more taut.

All the viols are "fretted" with gut, which is tied round the

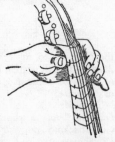

*Position of the Left Hand
on the Treble Viol*

36

neck at each half-tone. When the strings are stopped, the fingers are placed immediately behind the frets, pressing the strings towards the finger-board, so that the vibrating portion of the strings is between the bridge and the frets (not the fingers). This gives the stopped notes the sound quality of an open string.

The Viola d'Amore is a tenor viol, and is played like a violin, usually with fourteen strings : seven stopped and seven " sympathetic", which are made of fine steel or brass, and pass under the finger-board and through the bridge.

The Viola d'Amore

There are many different tunings : the following is given as an example :

37

PLUCKED INSTRUMENTS

The Egyptian Harp

THE HARP (Pl. 10)

In the early years of Queen Victoria's reign, when drawing-room music was the fashion, it was not unusual for a man of taste to play the flute, accompanied by his daughter or sister on the harp, for the harp was an instrument warranted to display her airs and graces, both musical and non-musical, to the best advantage! With its triangular shape and gracefully curved neck, the harp is an elegant-looking instrument. The strings are plucked by the fingers, and the resultant vibrations are amplified by the soundboard. The frame is made of sycamore wood,

38

the sound-board is of pine. The pegs holding the lower ends of the strings are held in a strip of beech (or other hard wood), which is glued along the centre of the sound-board. The tuning-pins round which the upper ends of the strings are wound pierce the wrest-plank which forms the upper part of the neck.

Most of the strings are of gut, and they are coloured according to their pitch-name to help the player to find them more easily. The eight lowest strings are of either metal or silk, over-spun with fine wire. They are tuned in the diatonic scale of C flat major, extending over six and a half

octaves, from two octaves below : ♯♭ to two

octaves above : ♯♭

By a system of pedals each string can be raised in pitch by a half or a whole tone (e.g. all the C flats to C, and all the Cs to C sharp, working on one pedal).

Chords and arpeggio figures sound well (*arpa* is Italian for harp), and the swishing, swirling sound produced by sliding the fingers across the strings is known as *glissando*.

The harp needs constant tuning, and before an orchestral concert the harpist can be seen busily tuning before the rest of the players have assembled.

It seems that the harp had its origin in prehistoric times, and might have come from the stretched string of an archer's bow, other strings of varying length (and pitch) being added, much in the same way as reeds or whistles were bound together to make a *syrinx* or pan pipes. The earliest evidence of a harp comes from Egypt and dates from the 13th century B.C.

THE HARPSICHORD FAMILY

The harpsichord was the most important of the keyboard instruments during the 16th, 17th and 18th centuries, holding a position analogous to that of the pianoforte of today. Three distinct instruments belong to the harpsichord family: *the virginal* (or *virginals*), the *spinet*, and the *harpsichord* proper.

Fundamentally they are all harps placed horizontally, with their strings plucked by plectra operated from a keyboard. When a key is de-

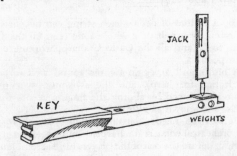

pressed by the player's finger, a " jack " made of wood rises, causing the plectrum (a quill or small piece of leather) to rise and pluck the string;

PL. 9. *Wilma Neruda (1839–1911), violinist, and wife of Sir Charles Hallé, the Conductor*

Pl. 10. *The Harp* (p. 38)

Pl. 11 (Right). Above *the Virginal* (p. 41). Below
the Spinet (p. 42)

PL. 12. *The Clavichord* (p. 53)

when the key is released, the jack falls, and the plectrum, which is fixed to a movable tongue of wood in the jack, slides silently past the string. When the jack comes to rest, a small tongue of felt automatically "damps" the string (stops it vibrating). This jack was the original "Jack-in-the-box".

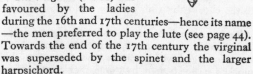

Metal strings are used, the lower ones being over-spun with wire.

The Virginal (Pl. 11) was favoured by the ladies during the 16th and 17th centuries—hence its name —the men preferred to play the lute (see page 44). Towards the end of the 17th century the virginal was superseded by the spinet and the larger harpsichord.

The case is rectangular, and the strings are at right angles to the keys. Each note has one string, and the sound is "twangy", and no alteration in quality is possible.

Its compass: [musical notation] could be extended

down by means of the "short octave"; the lowest G sharp being tuned to E, the F sharp to D, and the bottom note E to C. At the close of the 17th century a more complete chromatic compass was required, and some instruments can be seen to this day with the lowest G sharp and F sharp keys cut across, the back half giving the sharp and the front half the natural in the short octave.

English virginal music is of great importance in the history of music, as it demonstrates the earliest development of keyboard technique.

Up to the end of the 17th century the term "virginals" was loosely used in Britain to mean virginals, spinet or harpsichord.

The Spinet (Pl. 11) is similar to the virginals, in that it has one string to each note, but it is wing-shaped instead of being rectangular. The strings are set at an angle of about forty-five degrees to the keyboard. It was a domestic instrument which was in use from the latter half of the 17th century to the end of the 18th century. No alteration in tone-quality is possible.

Today a small harpsichord is coming into use. It is similar to the spinet, but it has two pedals: the *crescendo*, which causes the strings to be plucked more strongly by the leather plectra, thus producing a louder tone; and the *harp*, which changes the tone-quality by damping the strings with felt. The present-day spinet or small harpsichord, is known as a *triangle* or *triang*. The legs are detachable, and the instrument can be easily transported. The keyboard has a chromatic compass of five octaves:

The Clavicytherium was a spinet with strings perpendicular to the keyboard.

The Harpsichord (Pl. 17) is the largest instrument in this family, and it looks rather like the modern concert grand piano. There are two or more strings to each note, and they are set at right angles to the keyboard. The normal compass of the harpsichord is the same as that of the spinet.

To produce variety in tone colour and resonance, it is necessary to use mechanical devices, because by finger-touch alone so little difference can be made. By means of stops—similar to those on an organ—or by pedals, the number of strings to each note engaged in performance can be controlled. Similarly, the quality of tone can be changed to resemble that of a lute or a harp. In 1769 Tschudi (or Schudi) of London added the "Venetian swell", which was worked on the principle of the Venetian blind and which could control the volume of tone by the opening and closing of shutters placed over the strings and operated by a pedal.

It seems that the double (two-manual) keyboard instrument was favoured in Britain and Germany, while the single manual was more popular in Italy. Today the harpsichord can frequently be heard, and both types are in use. Many of the old instruments of the harpsichord family have been very carefully renovated, and they are being used as they were originally intended, no longer being silent museum specimens. New instruments are also being made by enthusiastic and highly-skilled craftsmen who are carrying on the traditions of the 17th and 18th centuries.

THE LUTE (Pl. 13)

The origin of the lute and other instruments with similar-shaped bodies, such as the rebec, the mandore and the mandoline, can be traced back into the distant past to the Oriental type of instru-

A Medieval Lute-player

ment whose body was made from a gourd, or half a gourd covered with a stretched skin. The name lute comes from the Arabic words *El Oud*, meaning instrument of wood.

By the 17th century the lute had acquired

twenty-six to thirty strings, and the tuning and adjusting of them was an expensive pastime both in time and money. During the 16th and 17th centuries it became very popular, and although it was the most difficult of stringed instruments to play, much music was composed for it.

The smallest lute, the *mandore* (or *mandora*), was used by the travelling minstrels on the Continent from the 12th to the 14th centuries, and there is evidence of its use in England during the 15th century. At this time another instrument which could be carried beneath a cloak appeared; this form survives as the mandoline.

The strings of the lute are plucked with the fingers, and they are duplicated in unison. The vibrating length of string extends from the top of the finger-board to the sound-board, and there is no bridge. The finger-board has frets of gut placed at each half-tone (as in the viols). An elaborately carved disc of ivory or wood is usually inserted in the circular sound-hole. The sound-board is of pine-wood, and the pear-shaped back is made from fine strips of English maple or sometimes from ivory and ebony, which are glued together.

The Archlute, the largest member of the family, has a double peg-box, so that some of the strings are not over the finger-board and can only be played as " open strings ". The *Theorbo* is similar to the archlute, but it is smaller.

A special notation called *Tablature* was used for all lute music, showing the string and fret to be used for each note, with its duration indicated

45

An Elizabethan Archlute

above by small marks similar to the " tails " of our modern staff notation.

The Mandoline has a pear-shaped body similar to the lute. The frets and strings are of metal. The eight strings are tuned in pairs to E, A, D, G (as on the violin) ; they are plucked with a plectrum of tortoiseshell held between the thumb and first finger of the right hand.

The Cittern was associated with the Church during the 15th century, but it was ousted by the superior attractions of the lute. Later it

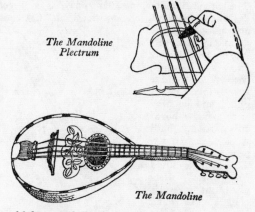

*The Mandoline
Plectrum*

The Mandoline

could frequently be found hanging in taverns and barbers' shops for the amusement of waiting customers. The strings of metal were tuned in pairs and were plucked with the fingers. Music for it was printed in tablature.

The Guitar is of great antiquity, having originally come to Europe through the Moors in Spain.

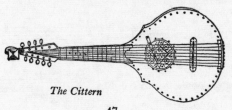

The Cittern

47

The Spanish guitar, popular today, is a direct descendant of the lute and cittern. Its flat back and sides are made of maple, ash, service or cherry wood; its sound-board, with a decorative sound-hole, is of pine; and its neck and finger-board are of some hard wood, such as ebony, pear-wood or beech. The finger-board has metal frets placed at intervals of half tones. Metal screws instead of rose-wood pegs are used for tuning the strings, of which there are six: three of gut and three of silk over-spun with silver wire. Today some of the upper strings are made of nylon.

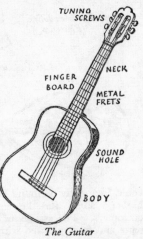

The Guitar

The Guitar is tuned thus:

but the notes are written thus:

48

PL. 13.   *An Elizabethan Lute-player*
(*The Lute*—p. 44)

PL. 14. *The Hurdy-gurdy or Vielle* (p. 55)

For performance in remote keys the *capo tasto* (or *cejuela*) is clamped on the finger-board, and raises the pitch of all the open strings.

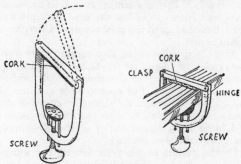

The Capo Tasto

The Banjo (Pl. 15) is of the same type as the guitar, but its body is open, and the resonator is of parchment stretched over a metal hoop. It is supposed to be of African origin, and was used by the slaves in the southern states of North America. In the 19th century it was the accepted instrument of the "nigger minstrels".

HIT INSTRUMENTS

The Pianoforte

About the year 1709 Cristofori, in Florence, produced a *gravicembalo col piano e forte*—a harpsichord with soft and loud. In this instrument the strings were not plucked, but were hit by hammers. The loudness and softness of the notes produced could be directly controlled by the amount of force exerted by the player's fingers on the keys. Earlier attempts at such an improvement had been made, but the new principle was not established until the production of Cristofori's instruments.

At the beginning of the 18th century there were two types of domestic keyboard instruments: the harpsichord and the clavichord, which, despite its very small tone, had considerable qualities of expression. Through the desire to combine the tone of the harpsichord with the less mechanical and more expressive qualities of the clavichord, the pianoforte was evolved.

By the middle of the 18th century the square piano was produced, and it quickly became very popular. In size and shape it was like the virginal. Some models were made to look like tables, and were fitted with drawers for music. (In sales catalogues today they sometimes appear wrongly labelled " spinet ".)

At the beginning of the 19th century the familiar Upright piano was produced. In this kind of instrument the strings, mounted on a metal frame, extend below the level of the keyboard.

Today several sizes of grand piano are in use, ranging from the Baby Grand, only four feet long, to the full Concert Grand, which is eight and a half feet long. Many experiments and improvements were made in the construction of the piano, but it was not recognised as an independent instrument until the end of the 18th and the beginning of the

19th centuries, when composers such as Weber and Beethoven, to mention only two, were writing specially for it.

If the panel, immediately above the keyboard of an upright piano, be removed, it will be seen that when the finger depresses a key it brings a hammer (covered in felt) into operation. This immediately moves forward and strikes the strings, and then quickly rebounds. A small felt pad (the damper), which normally presses on the strings, is released at the moment of striking, so that the strings are allowed to vibrate freely until they come to rest, or until the finger releases the key, which immediately brings the damper back on the string. All this mechanism is called the action. The sound is similarly produced in a grand piano.

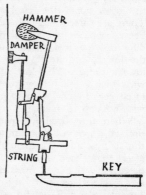

If the lower panel under the keyboard be removed, the iron frame will be seen, on which metal strings are stretched; they are fixed at their top ends to tuning-pins, which the tuner turns with a tuning-hammer when he restores the strings to their correct pitch.

Behind the strings is a varnished board. It is

of very thin pine, and is the sound-board or resonator, amplifying the sound of the strings and enhancing their tone-quality.

The shorter and thinner strings on the right-hand side produce the higher notes (the treble), and they gradually become longer and thicker for the lower notes (the bass) on the left-hand side. There are three strings to each of the higher notes, because one or two would be insufficient to produce the required amount of tone, then two for the lower, and finally only one for each of the lowest notes. The low strings are over-spun with thick wire; if they were not they would need to be very much longer to produce the low notes with enough resonance.

When the sustaining pedal, on the right, is pressed down, all the dampers are released from the strings, allowing them to continue to vibrate after they have been struck. When the soft pedal, on the left, is pressed down, the hammers are brought nearer to the strings, so that they cannot strike with such force. In a grand piano the hammers are automatically shifted, so that only one string out of three is struck. Hence the terms *una corda* (one string) when the pedal is depressed, and *tre corde* (three strings) when it is released.

The normal pitch range is seven, or seven and a quarter octaves extending from two octaves below:

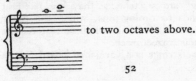

to two octaves above.

The Clavichord (Pl. 12)

The clavichord is contained in a rectangular box with the strings placed at right-angles to the keys. Each string is made to sound not by a plectrum, as in the harpsichord type of instruments, but by a metal tangent which hits the string and presses against it. On hitting the string, the tangent divides it into two lengths, one of which is free to vibrate, while the other is permanently damped by a piece of felt. The tangent not only sets the string in vibration, but it also determines the pitch of the note by "stopping" the string. The tangent in "stopping" the string has the same effect on the string as the player's left-hand fingers have on the strings of a violin, or guitar, or any other similar instrument.

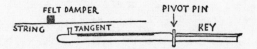

In clavichords made before about 1725 one string was made to serve two or more adjacent keys, thus economising on the number of strings in the instrument. Such an arrangement was possible, since the respective tangents to these adjacent keys could be placed along the same string, to produce the required pitch. These adjacent notes could not, of course, be sounded together; but then they were rarely needed thus, so the arrangement worked quite well.

Clavichords of this type were called *Fretted* in England and *Gebunden* (bound) in Germany.

The tone-quality is small and delicate. By agitating the depressed key, a kind of " vibrato " can be produced. In so doing the player can prolong the note. The clavichord is the only stringed keyboard instrument on which such an effect is possible.

The clavichord was popular from about the 15th century to the beginning of the 19th century, when it gave place to the pianoforte. Interest in its revival is now growing, and some very fine instruments are being made and played.

In Bach's time the compass of the clavichord was:

OTHER STRINGED INSTRUMENTS

The Dulcimer is a shallow, closed wooden box strung with wires which are hit with small wooden hammers. It was used mostly in puppet plays in the 17th and 18th centuries in England. There is also mention of it in English literature as early as the 15th century. Today it is used in gipsy bands of Eastern Europe, where it is called the **Cymbalum** or **Zimbalon**.

The Psaltery, a very old type of instrument, is similar to the dulcimer, but the strings are plucked with the fingers or with a plectrum. Known as the *Kin* in China, it has existed there for thousands of years. From Asia Minor, the many-stringed psaltery found its way westward into Europe, where it was known during the Middle Ages as the *Cythera barbarica*.

It might be said that the dulcimer was the forerunner of the piano-forte, and the psaltery was the forerunner of the harpsichord.

The Zither is an elaborate kind of psaltery, played in the Tyrol and adjoining mountainous districts. The player places it on a table and plays a melody on some of the strings, "stopping" them with his left thumb and plucking

The Dulcimer

them with a plectrum on his right thumb, while he plays an accompaniment on some of the other strings with the fingers of his right hand.

The Hurdy-gurdy or Vielle (Fr.) (Pl. **14**) is a stringed instrument of the violin type, with the strings set in vibration by a resined wooden wheel, turned by the player's right hand, while his left-hand fingers press keys not unlike those of the piano. There are six strings, the two outside ones being tuned to the keynote of the piece and sounding continuously, thus forming a drone similar to the bagpipes.

An Ancient Psaltery

CHAPTER III

WIND INSTRUMENTS

ALL WIND instruments are made to sound by causing air to vibrate inside a hollow tube. Part of this tube must be open, so that the air inside the tube has contact with the surrounding air. The inside of the instrument, known as the bore, may be cylindrical (the same width throughout its length) or conical (small at one end and gradually increasing in width to the other), or it may be cylindrical for part of its length and conical for the remainder. The hollow tube may be straight or curved.

The choice of material for a wind instrument depends on a number of factors, such as its ability to stand the strain imposed on it during the various processes of its manufacture, its durability, its capacity for being bent or coiled, and its weight. The instrument when finished must be hard and rigid and the inside of the tube must be smooth.

Wind instruments were played in very ancient times, in fact, remains of bone flutes of the Later Stone Age have been found. We know from the Bible that the flute was played in Hebrew religious processions, with drums, tambourines and cymbals, and a ram's horn was blown on special occasions.

Over 3,000 years ago the Egyptians used trumpets on ceremonial occasions and later the Greeks, at the Pythian games, were holding contests for solo playing on the aulos, a double-reed instrument, related to the oboe. The Romans, too, had a kind of oboe, and tubas of different sizes.

Since early times wind instruments have been gradually modified and improved and the orchestral instruments of today are almost as perfect as they can be for our present needs; but there is no knowing what further changes might be made, if, for instance, composers were to demand instruments with quarter-tones.

Wood-wind and Brass

Wind instruments are divided into two classes, the *wood-wind* and the *brass*. The term *wood-wind* does not signify that all the instruments in this class are made of wood; in fact, some are of ivory, of metal and of ebonite. Nor does the term *brass* mean that all these instruments are made of brass; there are some of silver, of copper, horn, ivory—and even wood!

The families of instruments generally regarded as wood-wind are:

> Flute
> Oboe
> Clarinet
> Saxophone
> Bassoon

The brass instruments are:

Horns
Trumpets
Cornets
Trombones
Tubas

This classification is based on the method of production of the sound. No sound will be made by simply blowing through the tube : a generator must be used. There are three types of generators : the *free air-reed*, the *cane-reed* and the *lip-reed*.

If the sound is generated by *air-reeds*, as in the flute, or *cane-reeds*, as in the oboe or clarinet, the instrument is wood-wind.

If the sound is generated by the vibration of the lips against a cup- or conical-shaped mouth-piece, the instrument is brass.

The Free Air-reed

(*a*) A compressed stream of air from the player's lips is directed against the edge of a mouth-hole (the embouchure) in the upper side of the tube. Transverse flutes, piccolos and pipes are played in this way.

An Elizabethan Flute Player

59

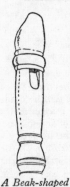

A Beak-shaped Mouth-piece

(b) Instead of the air-stream being directed straight from the player's mouth on to a mouth-hole, it can be driven through a channel in a beak-shaped mouth-piece and directed automatically against the sharp edge of a sound-hole. Recorders (flutes-a-bec), flageolets and "tin-whistles" are played in this way.

The Cane-reed

There are two types of cane-reed: the double, used for playing the oboe and bassoon, and the single, used for playing the clarinet and the saxophone.

(a) The double-reed consists of two small pieces of cane shaved thin at one end. At the thicker end they are bound together over a small metal tube called the staple. The paper-thin ends of the reeds are pressed almost flat together, but a small gap is left between them, which is made narrower by the player's lips when he sets the reeds in vibration, by blowing through them. The lower part of the staple is larger, and it is covered in cork so that it fits tightly into the end of the instrument. The staple is replaced by the "crook" in the bassoon.

(b) The single-reed is a flat piece

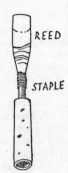

REED

STAPLE

The Double-reed

60

of cane shaved thin at one end. The thicker end is clamped by the " ligature " to the flat side of a beak-shaped mouth-piece. The thinner end lies over a narrow channel in the mouth-piece, so that the reed can vibrate when the player forces a stream of air between the reed and the mouth-piece.

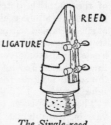

REED

LIGATURE

The Single-reed

The Lip-reed

The lips (almost closed) vibrate as reeds against a cup- or cone-shaped mouth-piece. The vibration set up is conveyed to the air in the tube of the instrument through the " throat " or neck of the mouth-piece. The quality of the tone produced depends on the shape of the mouth-piece ; for instance, the " brassy " bright tone is produced from a shallow cup, while a more mellow, veiled tone requires a deep cone. The smaller the mouth-piece in circumference, the higher the sounds which can be easily produced.

A Shallow Mouth-piece

A Deep Mouth-piece

The Pitch

On a wind instrument the pitch

of the sound is determined by the frequency or rate of vibrations which are set up in the column of air contained within the tube of the instrument. It is a natural law that a column of air can be made to vibrate at certain frequencies only. This means that only one series of sounds can be produced so long as the column of air remains the same length.

The wind-player can produce these sounds by varying the intensity of the air-stream. This he does by varying the pressure of his lips : the more he tightens them, the more compressed will the air-stream be, increasing the rate of vibration, and so producing notes of higher pitch. He slackens his lips in order to produce notes of lower pitch. The lowest possible note he can produce from a tube is the fundamental ; this and the higher ones—the octave, twelfth, double-octave and so on—are known as the harmonics.

The following series of notes can be produced on a tube about eight feet long :

If the tube were shorter, the sounds would all be relatively higher, so that a tube about four feet long would produce the following sounds :

If the tube were longer, say about eight feet six inches, these sounds would be available :

and so on.

The pitch of the notes in black is slightly flat, compared with the corresponding notes on a keyboard.

The entire harmonic series is contained within any tube, but it is not humanly possible to produce all the notes, owing to the extent of lip-pressure which would be needed. The width of the tube in proportion to its length is the factor determining the number of playable sounds. A wide-bored tube will sound its fundamental easily, and if it is not too wide, some of the lower harmonics as well. A narrower-bored tube might not sound the lowest two notes, but it will sound those above to the sixteenth note.

The wood-wind instruments are wide in bore compared with their length; only the fundamental and octave, or, as in the clarinet, the fundamental and twelfth, sound easily; but the brass-wind instruments are narrow in bore compared with their length, and so the middle and higher harmonics are easier to produce. This is the essential difference between the wood-wind and the brass-wind instruments.

The number of playable sounds which could be produced without the use of holes on a wood-wind

instrument would therefore be very limited.
If, however, a hole be bored in the tube, the
sounding length is shortened, as the boring of the
hole has approximately the same effect as cutting

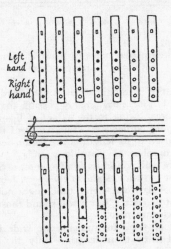

the length of tube off at the position of the hole.
It will be seen, then, that by having a number of
holes which can be covered by the fingers, the
sounding length can be varied by the player.
The shorter the tube, the higher the pitch of
the fundamental will be.

The octave above these notes can be obtained
by the player using the same fingering but blowing

PL. 15. *The Banjo* (p. 49)

harder (see p. 19), except on the clarinet, which sounds the twelfth instead of the octave.

WOOD-WIND INSTRUMENTS
Free Air-reeds

THE TRANSVERSE FLUTE FAMILY

The family of transverse (or German) flute is the highest in pitch of the wood-wind instruments.

The flute and piccolo are the only orchestral wind instruments which are held sideways. The higher notes of a flute can be shrill, and the lower ones can sound " hollow ". The flauto piccolo, the small flute, plays an octave higher than the concert flute. The piccolo has a bright, piercing tone, and is usually used for some particularly brilliant sound effect in the orchestra.

E 65

One flute can hold its own quite easily against all the strings in an orchestra, and for this reason it is a " solo " orchestral instrument. Usually there are two flutes, each playing its own part, but occasionally both play the same part.

Some composers require more than two flutes in their works. When a piccolo is wanted, one of the flautists usually plays it.

The concert flute is made of silver or hard wood or ebonite. The sound is produced by the player blowing across the mouth-hole, which is elliptical in shape and about half an inch in length. The tube is plugged with a cork or stopper at one end, and it is made " open " again by the mouth-hole, bored quite close to the stopped end of the tube.

The flute has a pitch range

The Piccolo

The flauto piccolo or piccolo has a compass of two octaves and five notes from and good players can produce one or two notes higher.

The Flute

The flute is one of the oldest wind instruments. In prehistoric times a reed or tube was blown across one open end. In the Middle Ages a cylindrical tube with six finger-holes was closed at one end, and the sound was produced by blowing across a side mouth-hole in the same manner as the flute of today.

From 1675 to 1775 the flute was made with a conical bore, and a key was added. In addition to the sounds produced by lifting the fingers successively for the primary scale, chromatic notes could be played by a system of " cross-fingering " ; by so doing the sound could be flattened by half a tone if the hole below the last open hole were closed by the finger.

The flute was made in the tonality of D—that is, the primary scale was D major. All chromatic notes could be produced by " cross-finger-ing ", as described above, except the semitone below bottom E. The D sharp key was therefore added to produce this note, and the flute was known as the one-keyed flute.

The One-keyed Flute

Up to 1850 as many as eight keys were added, but the one-keyed flute still held its own, and it became a very popular instrument among amateurs in this country. The tone produced by " cross-fingering " was not as clear as that on the notes of the primary scale.

Theobold Boehm (1793 or 4–1881) realised that there was room for much improvement in the construction of the flute. He was skilled in handling metal, as he had been trained in his father's business as a jeweller. He was a keen and accomplished flute-player, and also had knowledge of the science of sound. In 1830 he produced an improved type of flute, but he still used the conical bore.

In 1847, however, he began making flutes with cylindrical bore, and revolutionised the whole structure of the flute. This type is used today, and on it very decorative, quick passages can be played with comparative ease.

It was for the simple conical one-keyed flute of the 18th century that Bach, Handel, Haydn and Mozart wrote.

Flutes are used in military bands, but they are built in E flat, F, and B flat instead of D as the concert flute.

The Fife

This name is given to the B flat flute whose primary scale is B flat, and it is the chief instrument of the Fife-and-Drum band. The earlier models were of cylindrical bore, and were very out-of-tune. This model has, however, been superseded by the conical-bore type. It is between the concert flute and the piccolo in pitch. The modern type has up to as many as six keys.

The Flute d'amour has the same pitch as the oboe d'amore. Both these instruments were reputed to have a fascinating, smooth quality in their tone—hence their name. It is a minor third lower than the concert flute.

The Alto Flute sounds a fourth lower than the concert flute. It has a different appearance from the flute, as the head-joint is turned back on itself to simplify the fingering.

The Bass-flute is an octave lower than the concert flute, but it has never been much used.

The term bass-flute is sometimes wrongly given to the alto-flute. The flute in B flat, an octave lower than the fife, is sometimes called the bass-flute.

THE WHISTLE FLUTES

(Free Air-reeds, *continued*)

The Recorder (Pl. 19, 20)

The recorder has had many names in the course of its history. During the 18th century it was known in England as the English or Common Flute. In Germany it was called the Blockflöte. In France it was the Flûte Douce or the Flûte-a-bec, and in Italy, the Flauto Dolce. References to the recorder are numerous in the works of Shakespeare, Bacon, Milton, and other writers of the period.

During the 16th and 17th centuries the recorders were made in a number of sizes, and varied in length from a few inches to over four feet. Sets of these instruments containing from three to eight in varying sizes were used for playing in consort. These early recorders were made in one piece, and were lacking in any decoration. Those made during the late 17th and early 18th centuries were jointed and became more elaborate.

The sound is produced by the player blowing a stream of air through a small channel in the beak-shaped mouthpiece, which is directed against the sharp edge of the sound-hole. Recorders are often made in three sections, called joints. The bore of all recorders is conical, with the widest part at the mouthpiece end (in the head-joint), and tapering in the middle joint towards the lower end (the bell-joint).

There are six finger-holes, and a thumb-hole used in the production of notes above the octave, and there is an extra hole at the lower end to extend the pitch down a whole tone.

During the 17th century both the horizontal or German flute and the recorder were used in the orchestra, and Purcell, Scarlatti and Lully wrote for both instruments. During the first half of the 18th century Bach, Handel, Telemann and other composers included the recorder in their orchestral works.

With the growing sonority of the orchestra during the 18th century, the quiet, rather expressionless " hollow " tone of the treble recorder which was commonly used, was found to be inadequate, so the horizontal flute was more favoured and the recorder gradually became obsolete.

Today the recorder is regaining popularity, and it is being used in the performance of works originally intended for the recorder. Many fine instruments are being made, too. There are five sizes now in use: the Sopranino, which is the smallest and which is not used as much as the others; the Descant, or Soprano; the Treble, or Alto; the Tenor and the Bass. All the instruments have a compass of about two octaves above the following lowest notes:

Sopranino   Descant   Treble   Tenor   Bass

With the revival of the recorder a large quantity of music, both new and old, is now being published, both here and abroad.

The Flageolet

The flageolet differs from the recorder in detail only. The French type has four finger-holes on top and two holes underneath for the two thumbs. It survives in dance-music, and it is rare for this now. The English flute or flageolet, a somewhat similar instrument, appeared at the end of the 18th century. It has an ivory mouthpiece, and the six holes lie along

The Flageolet

71

the top of the pipe. It was about eighteen inches long.

The Double Flageolet

Two flageolets were bound together, or two holes were bored in a single piece of wood, so

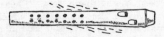

that the player could play more than one note at a time. It was popular among amateurs during the first half of the 19th century.

The Tabor-pipe

The pipe and tabor have been used for the accompaniment of the Folk-dance since the Middle Ages. The player plays this pipe with the fingers of his left hand, and beats a small drum (the tabor) suspended under his left arm, with a stick held in his right hand. There are three note-holes, two for the first and second fingers and one underneath for the thumb near the lower end of a narrow-bored, cylindrical tube. By using harmonics, fingerings and cross-fingerings, tunes within a compass of about an octave and a half can be played.

An 18th-century Dancer, with Pipe and Tabor

CANE-REEDS—DOUBLE-REEDS

THE OBOE FAMILY

All the instruments in this family are of conical bore and are played with a double-reed.

The Orchestral Oboe

When all the six finger-holes are covered, the note ⟨music⟩ sounds. By lifting each finger successively, the scale of D major is produced as in the flute. The oboe of today has a chromatic compass : ⟨music⟩ The instrument, of African blackwood or ebonite, is made of three joints : the top joint, into which the staple carrying the reed is inserted, the middle joint, and the bell-joint.

The oboe has been through almost as many processes of alteration and modification as the flute. The reed, too, has changed from being comparatively large and wide, more like a bassoon reed, down to its present small and slender shape. The tone has consequently changed, from being rather loud and raucous to its penetrating reedy and appealing tone of today.

The Oboe

There are usually two oboes in a symphony orchestra, which either play two different parts or " double ", as in the case of the flutes. They can stand alone well against the strings.

The oboe is also used in military bands, and sometimes two other sizes are used : one smaller, playing a minor third higher, and a larger one playing a whole tone lower than the concert oboe.

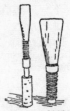

OBOE   BASSOON
Reeds of the Oboe and Bassoon

The double-reed type of instrument was used in prehistoric times, and there is evidence that it was used in Egypt, and in Greece, China, Hindustan, ancient America—in fact almost all over the world.

By the 16th century there were two families of double-reed instruments. The double-reed fitted to a *cylindrical* tube ; the Krummhorns belonged to this family, they were made in sets or " choirs " extending from bass to soprano, and were in general use during the 14th, 15th and 16th centuries in Europe. And the double-reed fitted to a *conical* tube ; these were Shawms or Schalmeys, and Pommers or Bombards, so called because of the buzzing sound on the lower

A 15th-century Krummhorn

74

notes. A choir or set of these instruments comprised two shawms (treble) the alto, tenor and bass pommer, and the double quint pommer.

In the 17th century the shawms and alto and tenor pommers were grouped together as *haut-bois*, to distinguish them from the large pommers, the *gros-bois*. The shawm became the oboe or hautbois early in the 17th century, and has been gradually developed into the concert oboe of today. The early hautbois, raucous and penetrating, were used in towns for open-air performances. They were also employed in military bands, first in France by Louis

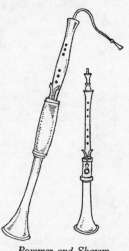

Pommer and Shawm

XIV, and later in England, where, with bassoons and percussion, they took the place of fife and drum bands, and remained during the 18th century.

The petty princelings of the 18th century were able to maintain their own chamber orchestras and armies, and it was a simple matter to bring their military musicians indoors. In this way the oboes came to be used, together with trumpets, in the orchestral works of Bach, Handel, Telemann, and their contemporaries.

The Cor Anglais or English Horn

This is an oboe sounding a fifth lower than the concert oboe. It is neither " English " nor a " horn "; the name is a corruption of *cor anglé* (angled horn), so called because the instrument is bent into a curve. The tube is longer than the oboe, and it ends in a globular or pear-shaped bell. The reed is inserted in a crook, which is bent at an angle for the convenience of the player. The tone colour is rather melancholy.

The Oboe d'Amore is rarely heard except in some of the works of J. S. Bach, in the Passion music and the Christmas Oratorio, for instance. It is built to play a minor third lower than the concert oboe (see Flute d'Amour).

The Oboe de Caccia (The Hunting Oboe)

J. S. Bach wrote parts for this in several of his works, including the Christmas Oratorio. It was a development of the alto pommer. As the oboe de caccia has become obsolete, the parts are now played on the cor anglais.

The Cor Anglais

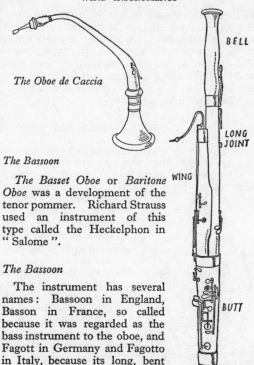

The Oboe de Caccia

BELL

LONG JOINT

WING

BUTT

The Bassoon

The Bassoon

The *Basset Oboe* or *Baritone Oboe* was a development of the tenor pommer. Richard Strauss used an instrument of this type called the Heckelphon in "Salome".

The Bassoon

The instrument has several names: Bassoon in England, Basson in France, so called because it was regarded as the bass instrument to the oboe, and Fagott in Germany and Fagotto in Italy, because its long, bent tube looks rather like a bundle of sticks.

The ordinary bassoon as used in the orchestra today is about eight feet long, and the tube has to symphony developed, or an instrumental piece in a vocal work. Bach also used the term in some of his keyboard works.

SONATA (It.): Originally meaning music " sounded " (played), as distinct from cantata " music sung ". The title has been given to different forms at different periods.

A sonata is usually made up of several contrasting pieces called movements—similar to the old dance suites (which were sometimes called sonatas), but not in dance style. The Classical Sonata dating from Mozart and Haydn (second half of the 18th century) for one or two instruments, usually has four movements, with at least one in Sonata Form.

Usually the classical sonata structure is used for works for one or more players, e.g., string trios, quartets, quintets, etc., and piano ; concertos (for orchestra and a soloist) and symphonies (for orchestra).

SONATA FORM : Is also called *First Movement Form* because so many first movements of sonatas, symphonies, concertos and chamber works have this shape. There are three main sections in the movement :

(1) *The Exposition*, containing two " Subjects " in different keys, joined by a modulating passage, the Bridge. Then follows a Codetta (a little tail).

(2) *The Development*. In this section the composer uses and develops any of the material in the Exposition, bringing the

be bent back on itself so that the player can cover the finger-holes. As the instrument is made of wood, it is constructed in sections or joints which fit neatly together. There are four wooden sections or joints: the wing, the butt, the long joint and the bell; and there is one metal section called the crook, into which the double-reed is inserted.

The bassoon has a compass:

The bassoon plays the bass part in the wood-wind quartet of flute, oboe, clarinet and bassoon.

The pommers, bombards or brummers, as they were called, were the immediate predecessors of the bassoon, but as they were straight instruments, they did not acquire the name "fagotti" (bundles of sticks).

Like the other wind-instruments, the bassoons can hold their own in an orchestra against all the strings. There are often two bassoons in a symphony orchestra.

The *Double-bassoon* (Fr. Contrebasson, Ger. Doppel-fagott, It. Contra fagotto)

The Double-bassoon

78

plays one octave lower than the bassoon. It is a transposing instrument, the sounds produced being an octave lower than the notes indicated on the printed page.

THE BAGPIPE FAMILY

Although there are several types of bagpipe, all instruments have two characteristics in common : they are reed-pipe instruments, and they have a reservoir of air so that a continuous supply of air can be provided, thus fulfilling the same function as the wind-chest of an organ. The wind supply may be provided either by the player blowing through a valve-tube or by bellows under his arm. The melody is played on a *chanter*, which is a reed-pipe with finger-holes. There may be one or more additional reed-pipes, called *drones*, which can each produce only one note, the tonic, and also perhaps the dominant (doh and soh) of the key of the instrument. As the player's mouth is not in direct contact with the reed, overblowing, as in other instruments, is impossible, and consequently the compass of the instrument is limited.

An Early German Bagpipe

The bagpipe was apparently in use a thousand years before Christ, and it was widely used in

79

Europe during the Middle Ages. It is in use in many countries today, but as it is impossible to include all the varieties in this book, only the following will be very briefly described :

The Highland bagpipe, or Great pipe
The Lowland Scottish pipe
The Northumbrian pipe
The Irish pipe
The Musette

The Highland bagpipe is filled from the player's mouth. It has a chanter and three drones. Nine notes only (G—A) can be produced on the chanter, forming a scale approximating to the key of A with the C and F lower than normal pitch, and a natural G. This is essentially an out-of-doors instrument, and the piper walks while he plays.

The Lowland pipe is similar to the Highland pipe, but is bellows-filled.

The Northumbrian pipe is for use indoors, and has a softer, sweeter tone than the

The Highland Bagpipe

Scottish pipes. It is bellows-filled. The chanter produces the scale of G, and there are four drones tuned to G and D.

The Irish pipe as used today has a chanter, pro-

PL. 17. *The Harpsichord* (p. 43)

PL. 18. *Beethoven's Pianoforte*
(The Pianoforte—p. 49)

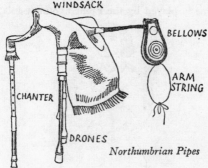

Northumbrian Pipes

ducing a soft pleasant tone,
and three drones. The
drones play C in three
octaves. By pressure of the
wrist on certain metal keys
a crude kind of Tonic-
Dominant (doh, soh) ac-
companiment can be pro-
duced on the three drones.

The piper sits to play,
with the bag under his left
arm and the bellows under
his right arm—they have to
be tied to his arm and his
body so that he can operate
them.

The Musette was a
bellows-type of bagpipe

*The Ancient Irish
War pipes*

F   81

originally played by the French country-folk, but

The Musette (Early 17th Century)

it became very popular in Court circles during and after the reign of Louis XIV (1645–1715).

CANE-REEDS—SINGLE-REEDS

THE CLARINET FAMILY

The clarinet consists of a cylindrical tube with a single beating reed. The tone is less nasal in quality than that of the oboe. Since the reed closes one end of the tube, the pipe becomes "stopped",

82

and it produces notes an octave lower than those produced from an open pipe of the same length. As it has a cylindrical bore, and is stopped at one end, it overblows at the twelfth.

The orchestral clarinet has a notational compass of nearly four octaves above

In a symphony orchestra the clarinetist usually has two instruments—one in A and another in B flat. (They are transposing instruments, see page 150.) The clarinet in C is not used, as its tone is inferior to the others. With improved technique, and instruments, there is a tendency for clarinetists to use only one instrument now, the B flat. Like other members of the wood-wind, there are usually two clarinets in a symphony orchestra.

The clarinet does not seem to have been used in the

The Clarinet

The Bass Clarinet

orchestra before 1720, and Mozart first used it in 1778 in the Paris Symphony, after having heard it in Mannheim earlier in the same year. The clarinet family is most important today in the Military Band, the higher instruments occupying the same position as the violin in the orchestra.

The Bass Clarinet, usually built in B flat, plays an octave lower than the clarinet. As it has such a long tube, the lower portion of it is curved upwards, and ends in a bell, and the upper end is bent downwards, so that the reed is within reach of the player's mouth.

The Basset Horn is a tenor instrument which has a similar appearance to the bass clarinet.

THE SAXOPHONE FAMILY (Pl. 22)

The Modern French Horn

The saxophone was invented by Adolphe Sax of Brussels in 1840. It is a hybrid instrument, having a single reed like the clarinet, a conical tube like the oboe, but it is of metal. Of the twelve different sizes which have been made, only two are in general use today—one is in B flat and the other is in E flat. (They are both transposing instruments, see page 150.) The saxophone is usually associated with dance-music, but several composers,

84

including Vaughan Williams in his ballet "Job", have included it in the orchestra for some special effect.

BRASS-WIND INSTRUMENTS

The Horn

The orchestral horn is known as the French Horn (Pl. 21). It is a brass instrument with a narrow conical tube, over eleven feet long, ending in a large bell, and having a funnel-shaped mouthpiece. There are two types of French horn: the Natural or Hand-horn, and the Valve horn. The notes of the harmonic series are available on brass instruments, but as the bore of the horn tube is so narrow compared with its length, it is impossible to produce the fundamental with any resonance of musical value.

Early in the 18th century, when the hunting-horn became an orchestral instrument, pieces of tubing of various lengths, known as crooks, were introduced. By inserting one of these into the

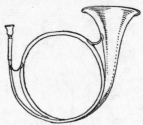

The Hunting Horn

tube, the total length of the vibrating air-column could be altered, thus altering the pitch of the fundamental and the corresponding harmonic series

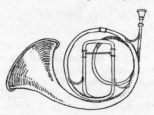

The Natural Horn with Crooks

above it. Contemporary orchestral parts show that horns in G, F, E flat, D and C were required. By inserting the G, F, E flat, D or C crooks, therefore, the corresponding harmonic series above each of these fundamentals could be sounded by the player. All horn parts were written in the key of C, and the treble clef was used except for those notes which extended into the bass clef, and these were written an octave lower than they sounded.

Horn in C alto :—
    notes available

Horn in F :—
    notes available.

A complete scale is not possible, and some notes are out of tune with the Tempered scale, but the player could adjust the pitch of these sounds by inserting his right hand into the bell of the instrument. These notes are known as " stopped " notes.

The French horn with valves is now used in the orchestra. Normally it is pitched in F. By means of valves, all the missing notes of the chromatic scale can be filled in ; operated by three fingers of the player's left hand, they instantaneously bring into use pieces of tubing which lengthen the air-column by a semitone, two semitones or three semitones, respectively, and as these valves can be used simultaneously, the air column can be extended as much as six semitones. For example, between the second and third harmonic there is a gap of six semitones; by playing the third harmonic by means of his lip-pressure, the player can get any of the six notes beneath it by means of his valves. The valve system was invented during the second decade of the 19th century, but the natural horn held its own until about the middle of the century. For some years both forms were used in the orchestra, but the natural horn had finally disappeared by the last quarter of the century. The early valve-horns were far from perfect, and for this reason they were ignored by composers until about 1835. Some Prussian military bands, however, had adopted them before 1830.

The German double-horn, which can be played in either F or B flat alto alternatively, by means of a valve, is gaining in popularity. The B flat alto form is favoured for the production of the higher notes.

The tone of the horns can be mellow: they blend well with the wood-wind. The tone can be subdued by the insertion of a mute into the bell, and by harder blowing the tone can sound harsh.

Originally the horn was the actual horn of some animal; later it still maintained its curved cone shape and was end-blown,

A Saxon Hunting Horn

although it was made of any hard substance. It was used for signalling of various kinds, especially in the communal life of the Middle Ages.

The later hunting-horns were much longer, so that more notes could be blown on them, and they were made circular so that they were easier to carry in the hunting field.

An Ancient Hunting Horn

THE TRUMPET FAMILY

The trumpet consists of a narrow tube, cylindrical for most of its length, which ends in a bell of medium size and which has a cup-shaped mouthpiece. The compass of the trumpet is higher than that of the horn, and the tone is brighter. The principle of the sound production is the same as for the horn.

The Modern Valve Trumpet—used in the orchestra today—is played on the same principle as the valve horn. It is pitched in B flat, but can be altered to A

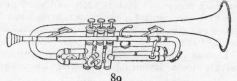

by means of a *rotary change valve*. Being four and a half feet long, it is only half the length of the old natural trumpets which were used until after Beethoven's time. There are usually three trumpets in a symphony orchestra.

The Natural Trumpet with crooks was used from the 17th century until nearly half-way through the 19th century.

The Natural Trumpet without crooks is now only used in England for ceremonial fanfares.

The Bach Trumpet

In Bach's time fewer crooks were used than later, and every orchestral trumpet-player would have four trumpets by his side : they were in G, F, D and B flat. By means of crooks he could lower the pitch of these by a tone or a semitone, and in some cases by muting he could raise the pitch by a semitone. By so doing he could play in any key, but he could only play the sounds of the harmonic series within that key.

The instruments in use then were twice as long as those used today, and the player was expected to be able to produce the harmonics in the fourth octave, where the notes lie scale-wise, as well as the lower sounds such as the second to the eighth harmonic. These high sounds (clarino parts) were not easy to get, and they required much practice and hard work for the player, even when he had a suitable lip, good teeth, breath control and bodily strength.

During the 19th century, when trumpet-players were favouring a shorter instrument, interest in Bach's music was increasing; but the players had lost the art of playing the higher notes, as on the old long trumpet, and found these trumpet parts very difficult to play on their own instruments. In 1884 a straightened valve trumpet with a conical mouthpiece was used, and became known as the Bach trumpet.

Now it is no longer considered necessary to use a straightened trumpet, and a folded instrument in high D is generally used.

The Slide Trumpet

Since about the middle of the 17th century attempts at various times have been made to produce natural trumpets with a sliding mechanism on the principle of the trombone (see page 92), but they have never been very successful, as the instruments were found to be much more difficult to play than the valve trumpets.

Slide trumpets were used, however, in town bands in Bach's time for the performance of chorales from the church tower at certain times. The treble part of a chorale lies below the series of harmonics which occur scalewise, so the gaps had to be filled in by means of the slide.

The history of the trumpet goes back to ancient times,

A Roman Buccina
(A kind of Tuba)

and it played an important part in early religious ceremonies, such as those described in the Bible. There is evidence that it was also used in battle by the Greeks and in processions by the Romans.

Henry VIII had forty-two instrumentalists, of whom fourteen were trumpeters. The trumpet

Ceremonial Trumpet

became a member of the orchestra at the beginning of the 17th century, and Purcell, Bach and Handel wrote florid solo parts. The trumpet becomes much less a melodic instrument, and the higher notes are no longer used in the works of Haydn and Mozart. Wagner made much use of the valve trumpet in his contrapuntal and chromatic style of composition.

THE TROMBONE FAMILY (Ancient name: Sackbut)

It has a tube of cylindrical bore ending in a medium-sized bell, and it has a cup-shaped mouthpiece. In these respects it is similar to the trumpet, but it differs from it by having a sliding arrangement instead of valves worked by pistons to extend the tube, and the mouthpiece is larger, which makes the tone less trumpet-like.

As in the horn and trumpet, the principle of harmonics is applied.

The Tenor Trombone, the most important member of the family, is nine feet long. In the first position its fundamental is B flat below the bass stave. It has a chromatic compass :

and by successive changes down to :

The Bass Trombone in its first position has as its fundamental either G or F one octave below the bass clef. Its chromatic compass extends from :

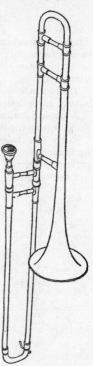

The Trombone

and by successive changes down to :

The actual fundamentals are not so easy to produce as the harmonics. They are spoken of as *pedal notes*, and are seldom if ever used on the bass trombone.

There are usually two tenor trombones and one bass in an orchestra.

A conical mute is occasionally used, as in the horn and trumpet.

With the tube at its shortest, the highest fundamental will be produced; with each successive extension of the sliding tube the fundamental will be lowered by a semitone. There are seven recognised positions, thus giving seven fundamentals and their respective harmonics.

It will be seen from this system that many notes can be produced in more ways than one, as a low harmonic on a lesser length (lower fundamental) or a higher harmonic on a greater length (higher fundamental). Intonation depends entirely on the player's judgment and

The 16th-century Sackbut

94

his ability to stop the slide where he wants it. The range of each position is about two octaves.

OTHER BRASS INSTRUMENTS

Cornet à Pistons

The cornet consists of a metal tube which is for the most part cylindrical in bore and for the rest conical. It has a cup-shaped mouthpiece, which

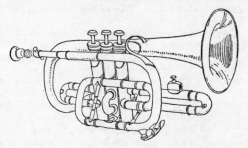

is usually deeper than that of the trumpet. The compass of the cornet is almost the same as that of the trumpet, and the gaps of the harmonic series are filled in by means of three valves. As the bore of the cornet is wider than that of the trumpet, the production of the notes is easier, and therefore greater flexibility in performance is possible. The tone has neither the brilliance of the trumpet nor the mellowness of the horn.

Nowadays the cornet is built in B flat, but it can be automatically changed to A by the player opening an extra short length of tubing by means of a *rotary transposing cylinder*.

The cornet came into being in France in about 1827. It was a development of the small horn known by several names, such as cornet simple, cornet de poste, or cornet ordinaire. The original cornet was about four feet long, and was built in C, but by means of coiled crooks it could be lowered in pitch by one, two, three or four semitones. The only notes of the harmonic series which were possible to play were 2, 3, 4, 5, 6, 7 and 8.

Since 1827 many alterations in the shape of the cornet have been made, but during the last fifty years very little change has taken place.

Because of the comparative ease with which it can be played, the cornet has been adopted in most European countries for use in military bands, brass bands and light orchestral music.

The Bugle is only used for military signalling. It consists of a brass or copper tube with wide conical bore, ending in a bell and having a cup-shaped mouthpiece. With these characteristics it is therefore related to the horn and the trumpet, but only a few notes of the harmonic series are playable.

An Early 19th-century Soldier with Bugle

Pl. 19. *A Recorder Consort* (p. 70)

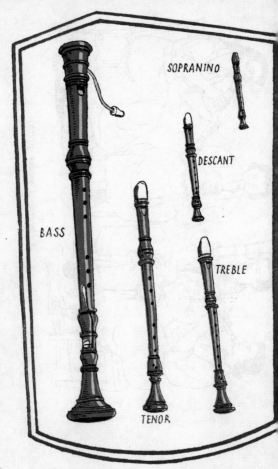

SOPRANINO

DESCANT

BASS

TREBLE

TENOR

PL. 20. *The Modern Recorder Family (p. 69)*

THE TUBA GROUP

The name " Tuba " is an omnibus word used nowadays for any brass instrument other than the trombones, which can play a bass part.

It will be remembered that neither the horn nor the trumpet could sound the fundamental note, because of the narrow bore of both these instruments. This means that for a horn in C, for instance, to sound its bottom note, the second harmonic (called the 8-*foot C*), the length of its tube must be sixteen feet, and thus half its length is practically useless. When the experiments on brass instruments were being made, to explore the possibilities of the use of

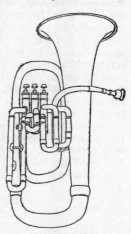

The Bass Tuba

valves, it was found that if the conical bore of a tube were made wide enough in proportion to its length, it was possible for the fundamental note to sound when a cup-shaped mouthpiece was used. This knowledge opened up many possibilities. The Germans classified brass instruments into *half-tube* instruments, that is, those instruments with narrow bore and therefore lacking the fundamental

G 97

note, such as horns and trumpets, and into *whole-tube* instruments, e.g., tubas, with wide bore and a playable fundamental note.

On the *half-tube* instruments it was found that three valves for filling in the missing notes between the notes of the harmonic series were all that were necessary, but on the *whole-tube* instruments there was a bigger gap to fill between the first and second harmonic. It was therefore found necessary to add a fourth valve, which, used on its own, would lower the pitch by two and a half tones, and in conjunction with the other three would fill in the entire gap between the octave, the distance from the first and the second harmonic.

The tuba used in the orchestra today is far from being a standardised instrument. In this country it is built in F, and is a development of the Military E flat tuba.

It has a compass of :

The *Bass Tuba* is the name given to the Bombardon when it is used in the orchestra.

The Military Tubas

The *Euphonium* is in B flat and has a compass :

E Flat Military Brass Bass has a compass:

B Flat Military Brass Bass or *Bombardon* has only three valves instead of four, so there is a gap between (1) and (2):

The Bombardon

The *Baritone* is similar to the euphonium, but it has a narrow bore and only three valves.

Wagner used what he called the " tenor tuba " and " bass tuba ", but they were really modified horns. His contrabass tuba had the same compass as the E flat Military Brass Bass (see above).

SOME OBSOLETE LIP-REED INSTRUMENTS

The Cornett

In remote times tusks and horns of animals were used both for making signals (such as the ancient hunting-horn), or for producing some sort of music. It was found that other notes

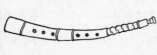

could be sounded by making holes, opened and closed by the fingers, in the side of the horn or tusk. In the Middle Ages an instrument of this type, the cornett, was being used. (This should not be confused with the cornet.) It was made of wood or ivory, but still retained the horn shape, and had a compass of about two octaves.

The Serpent (Pl. 25)

During the 16th century the serpent, a bass instrument of similar type, joined the family of cornetts. It was usually made of wood, and it had a conical bore, and was nearly eight feet long. As the tube was curved, the bore could not be drilled, as on a straight tube, so each section was made in transverse halves, which had to match exactly. After being glued together, they were bound with leather, and were sometimes further strengthened with metal bands.

The Russian Bassoon

The instrument had six finger holes, and was originally held vertically by the player, but this position was changed when the serpent was adopted for use in military bands, especially when on the march. Its lowest note was the fundamental.

The serpent survived for about 300 years, but

finally was ousted by the lower brass instruments in the modern orchestra.

The Russian Bassoon or *Bass Horn* was a metal serpent straightened out and doubled back so that it was easier to play in the military band on the march. The Russian bassoon was used in military bands until the middle of the 19th century.

Other instruments of the same type were the *Keyed Bugle* and the *Ophicleide*.

CHAPTER IV

PERCUSSION INSTRUMENTS

PERCUSSION INSTRUMENTS are members of an ancient instrumental family—perhaps the oldest. Some of its members still retain their primitive form in the modern orchestra.

Instruments of percussion have always been popular in Asia and Africa, and instruments from these continents have found their way into Europe at three different periods in history. It seems that during the 12th, 13th and 14th centuries the Crusades were responsible for bringing the kettle-drums (then called nakers) to Europe. During the 18th century the popularity of " Turkish music " in European armies introduced via Austro-

Hungary, caused the addition of a variety of percussive instruments. From the First World War,

A 17th-century Mounted Drummer

with the influence of American-negro music on dance-music, further additions have been made.

DRUMS

These are made of a skin stretched over a frame. There are several kinds of drums : the kettle-drum, the side-drum, the bass drum and the tenor drum. The tambourine is also a form of drum.

The Kettle-drums (timpani) are the only drums which can produce notes of definite pitch. A wooden hoop, over which a skin is stretched, is held in place by a circular iron ring mounted on a basin-shaped metal shell. By means of screws or "taps" placed round the shell, the tension on the skin can be adjusted for tuning the drum.

Drum-sticks of cane, with padded ends (heads), are used for hitting the drum to produce the sound.

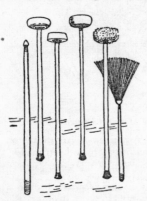

Sometimes side-drum sticks or sponge-headed sticks are used for special effects.

Two kettle-drums were used in the 18th-century orchestra, the larger drum with the range :

and the smaller :

The only notes which were required of the kettle-drums were the Tonic (doh) and the Dominant (soh) of the key of the composition being played. Since Beethoven's day, however, any pair of notes is used. During the 19th century three drums became the usual number required by composers, the following being the pitch range :

Other sizes have since been required for the performance of certain works, but they are exceptional. The low, middle and high drums are those which are normally in use today.

The Side-drum has a small cylindrical shell, or hoop, with parchment stretched over both ends. Over the lower end there are " snares " (strings stretched across, touching the parchment) to give a rattling sound when the drum is struck. On some side-drums the snares can be lifted clear of the parchment with a lever if the rattling sound is not required.

Two wooden drumsticks are used on the upper end of the drum. The side-drum is so called because it was slung to the player's side in military bands.

The 18th-century Military Side-drum

The Bass Drum (Pl. 24) the largest drum, has a narrow, cylindrical, wooden shell, covered at both ends with stretched vellum. It has a deep booming sound, which is produced with one stick with a large padded head. A single-headed bass drum which has vellum over one end only, is called a gong-drum.

The Tenor Drum is rarely used in the orchestra.

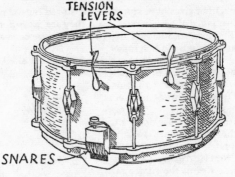

Orchestral Side-drum

It is midway in size between the side-drum and the bass drum.

The Tabor (see Pipe and Tabor).

The Tambourine is a small wooden hoop covered in over one end with stretched vellum.   Into the

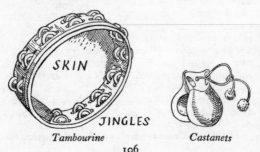

Tambourine   *Castanets*

hoop pairs of small metal discs, called *jingles*, are inserted so that they can vibrate freely when the tambourine is either shaken or hit with the knuckles or fingers of the player.

A 17th-century French Dancer with Tambourine

OTHER INSTRUMENTS WITH NO DEFINITE PITCH

The Triangle is a steel rod bent to form a triangle open at one angle. It is hung by a piece of string, which is held in the performer's hand or attached to a music-stand or to one of the drums. The triangle is hit with an steel *beater*.

Cymbals are plates of brass fitted with leather handles in the centre. Different effects can be produced: two plates can be clashed together, as on page 101, or rattled together at the edges, or one plate can be hit by a drum-stick of one kind or another.

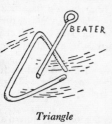

Triangle

Castanets are two pieces of hard wood shaped like scallop shells. The two shells are hinged with a piece of string, which is

107

Orchestral Castanets

*A Ballerina of the
1830's with Castanets*

looped over the finger and thumb of the performer. The castanets came originally from
Spain.

Sometimes two shells are hinged on a flat stick
of hard wood, and they are sounded by shaking the
stick. This type is used in the orchestra when there
is no time for the player to fix the string of the
other type over his fingers.

The Gong is a large, heavy disc of metal with
the edge bent, so that the disc looks like a dish.
The gong is suspended on a string, and is hit with
a soft-headed drum-stick.

Occasionally a *rattle* (like the old watchman's

rattle) or an *anvil* or a *Chinese block* are used, but these are rare.

INSTRUMENTS WITH DEFINITE PITCH

Tubular Bells are metal tubes of varying length hung on a wooden frame. There are usually

Tubular Bells

eight, forming a complete scale, and tunes can be played on them. A wooden mallet is used for striking the bells.

Celesta is a set of steel plates, each of which is attached to a wooden resonator, giving an ethereal quality to the tone. The sound is produced by hammers, which are operated from a small key-board.

Mustel invented the celesta in about 1880, and Tchaikovsky introduced it in his " Dance

The Celesta

of the Sugar Plum Fairy" in the Nutcracker Suite.

Glockenspiel is a set of steel plates played with two small hammers dulcimer-wise.

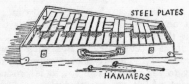

The Glockenspiel

Xylophone is a set of hard wooden bars played in the same way as the Glockenspiel.

CHAPTER V

THE ORGAN

THE ORGAN consists of a number of "whistle" pipes of varying lengths, mounted on a wind-chest, and they are made to sound by wind, which is supplied to the wind-chest by means of bellows. Each pipe produces only one sound.

The pipes are placed in rows or *ranks*, each rank supplying a complete range of notes of some particular tone-quality. So that all these ranks do not sound together, slides of wood pass under the tips of the pipes of each rank. When a particular rank is required, the slide controlling that rank is moved by the player pulling out a " stop ", so that holes, bored in the slide, coincide with the tips of the pipes.

Each note is fitted with a hinged lid, called a pallet, which seals the supply to the pipe until a key is depressed on a keyboard. The key is operated either by the player's finger (on a manual) or by the player's foot (on the pedal-board). When a key is depressed, the pallet, connected to the key by a series of rods called trackers and stickers, opens and allows the wind to pass through the pipe. The keyboards and stops are known collectively as *the console*.

Stops

The words " stop " and " register " can signify

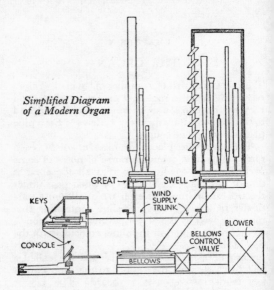

*Simplified Diagram
of a Modern Organ*

a rank or a set of pipes governed by one stop. In modern organs valves take the place of slides, and small balanced ivory levers are used instead of stops.

Most pipes are of the whistle variety and are made of wood or metal. Ranks of these are called *flue stops*.

Other pipes have at their base a tongue of metal which vibrates against a small brass tube called an

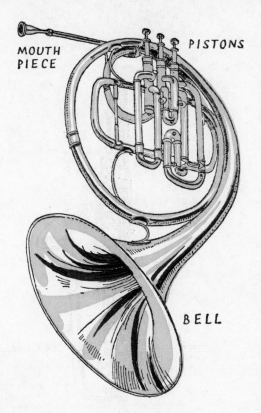

MOUTH
PIECE

PISTONS

BELL

PL. 21. *The French Horn* (p. 85)

KEYS

PL. 22.   *A Saxophone* (p. 84)

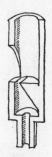

Reed Stop   *Flue Stop*

eschallot or a shallot. Ranks of these are called *reed stops.*

Flue Stops

The Eight-foot Stop brings into use pipes which sound at unison pitch, corresponding to the notes on a pianoforte keyboard.

The Four-foot Stop brings into use pipes sounding an octave above unison pitch.

The Sixteen-foot Stop brings into use pipes sounding an octave lower than unison pitch. There are also others, a two-foot stop and a thirty-two-foot stop, bringing into use pipes sounding correspondingly higher and lower than unison pitch.

The Mutation Stop sounds an interval above the unison, sounding G, E or C when the key C is depressed.

H   113

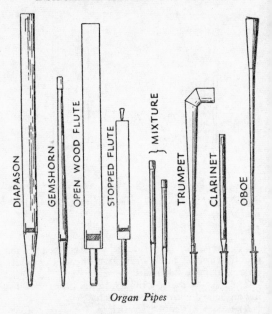

Organ Pipes

The Mixture Stop consists of ranks of mutations mixed together, thus adding brilliance to the tone.

The Diapason tone is the basic tone of the organ, and is obtained from an open metal pipe.

Stopped Diapasons are really flutes of broad tone. The term " stopped " here means that the pipe is closed at one end by a cover or stopper; with its use the tone quality is changed, and the pitch is lowered about an octave. Flutes are of wood or metal, and can be open or stopped.

The Bourdon, often a pedal stop, is a variety of stopped diapason.

String-toned stops are usually made of metal and have thin bodies.

To acquire the exact tone-quality which is desired, very subtle adjustments to the tone-producing portion of the pipe have to be made. This art of adjustment, known as *voicing*, is very skilled work, and can only be done by experts.

Reed Stops

There are many *reed stops*, which can imitate the tone-quality of orchestral reed and brass instruments. These different tone-qualities are produced by means of pipes of different " scale " —a term used to denote the difference in shape and diameter of the pipe tubes—by varying the wind-pressure, and by using various shapes and thicknesses of metal reeds.

Manuals

Each manual of an organ is almost a self-contained organ, and certain stops are associated with certain manuals. A large organ can have as many as five manuals.

The Great Organ is the basic manual, and has a Diapason chorus of various pitches : sixteen-foot, eight-foot, four-foot, two-foot and a mixture.

The Swell Organ has reeds as well as flute stops. The pipes are enclosed in a box fitted with shutters which are worked by a pedal. When these shutters are opened, the tone "swells", and when they are closed, the tone diminishes. The box is called the *swell-box*. Nowadays the swell-box is fitted to other manuals.

The Choir Organ has softer-toned pipes, and is used for accompanying.

The Solo Organ has stops comparable with solo orchestral instruments. These can be accompanied on another manual.

The Echo Organ is found on very large organs, and produces a distant sound-effect on very soft pipes.

The Pedal Organ. The pitch of the notes on this is an octave below that on the manuals. Its contribution to tone-quality is similar to that of the lowest-sounding orchestral instrument.

The specification on each manual varies with the size of the instrument.

The Materials of an Organ

Much of the organ is made of wood, which must be of high quality. It has to be seasoned for many years, both out of doors and in, so that it will withstand variations of humidity and temperature. If it is to be used in an organ abroad, it has to be specially treated so that it will withstand the ravages of insects. The best material for the metal pipes is " spotted metal "—a mixture of tin and lead. The pipes are made from sheet metal, which is joined by very fine soldering. For the bellows high-quality sheepskin leather is used. Ivory and ebony are used for the manual keys.

For the production of a first-class organ—as for any other instrument, for that matter—only the best materials are used, and highly skilled craftsmen are employed.

When an organ is required for a particular purpose, in a particular building, many factors have to be taken into consideration. Only after much thought and calculation can the required organ be designed. It is rare, therefore, for two organs to be identical.

Origin

The organ is said to have originated in Chaldea and Greece, where it first appeared as Pan Pipes or Syrinx. Reeds were cut off just below the knot, so that air blown down the reeds had to return to the open end. These were therefore stopped pipes producing a note nearly an octave below that produced on an open pipe.

Pan Pipes or Syrinx

By making a slit in the knot, and a notch with a bevelled edge in the pipe just above the knot, a sound could be made by blowing through the lower end of the reed. Thus the whistle-form of open pipe came into being.

The reed pipe, although used in bagpipes in ancient times, was not used in the organ until the 15th century.

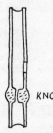

KNOT

The whistle pipes were placed on a wooden box, the wind-chest, and the wind was supplied by two people who blew through flexible tubes. Unless the pipes were stopped by the player's hands or fingers, all the pipes sounded together.

The slider was next introduced. Each pipe was governed by a slider which was perforated, so that, on being drawn in or out, the wind to the pipe could be admitted or excluded. Next came a leather bag as a reservoir for the air, and later primitive forge bellows were used.

The Roman Hydraulus or water-organ came into being during the 3rd century B.C. By using the weight of water, the wind-supply system produced equal wind-pressure in the reservoir. Pipes were made of bronze and copper. There is evidence of a water organ which was in use during the 1st century B.C. It had one and a half octaves, with keys and three ranks of pipes, and produced " Four-foot " pitch.

The organ was used for public feasts, and was not adopted for use in the church until A.D. 450, when it was apparently used in Spain. In the 7th century it was used in Rome to improve the singing of the congregation. The art of organ-making was known in England in the 8th century. In the 10th century there was a large organ at Abingdon Abbey and another at Glastonbury. Winchester Cathedral had a famous organ of 400 pipes of brass and copper. There were two organists ; probably one worked the levers to make the pipes sound, while the other worked the stop slides. Only one key at a time would have been used. The keys were three inches wide, and the organist was known as *pulsator-organum* (" organ-beater ") !

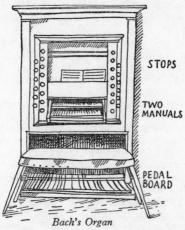

Bach's Organ

By the 14th century fixed organs came to be called *positif* or *positive*, in contrast to *portative* (portable) organs, which were, by this date, being used in processions in Germany and Italy. The keys were closer together by this time, and could be operated by the fingers of the player.

By the end of the 15th century the organ was developing into its modern form, with two manuals and a pedal-board. By the 16th century pipes of conical construction were in use, and the keys were small enough for an octave to be spanned by the player's hand (Pl. 26).

During the 18th century, Jordan, an Englishman, enclosed a section of the organ in a box with a sliding front, thus allowing the tone to swell or diminish, hence the term " swell-organ ".

A marked development in the mechanism of the organ was made during the 19th century, whereby " composition pedals ", worked by the foot, enabled selected and fixed combinations of stops to be drawn.

By developing the use of the pneumatic lever for operating heavy mechanism, the use of larger organs was made possible. More recently electric mechanisms have replaced the mechanical type, giving great control with less effort, allowing the organist to concentrate on the musical effect.

Since 1930 the electronic organ has been in use ; this has neither pipes nor wind, and it is claimed that by electrical production many tone-qualities can be produced at will. It occupies no more room than a grand piano, and is considerably cheaper than a pipe organ ; its installation requires little more than its connection to an electric power plug. The popularity of the pipe organ, however, seems to have been little affected by the electronic organ.

PART THREE

The Concert Programme

CHAPTER VI

TERMS IN COMMON USE

ABEND LIED (Ger.) : Evening song.

ABEND MUSIK (Ger.) : Evening music.

A CAPPELLA (It.) : Literally, *in the church style.* Unaccompanied vocal music.

ADAGIO (It.) : Slow.

AIR AND VARIATIONS : Usually a song-like melody, which is followed by varied treatment of itself either in melody, harmony or rhythm.

ALBUMBLATT (Ger.) : Literally, *album leaf*—a short, light instrumental piece.

ALLEGRETTO (It.) : Rather quick.

ALLEGRO (It.) : Literally, *lightly and brightly.* It now means quick.

ALLEMANDE (Fr.)
ALMAN (Eng.) } A moderately lively dance in four-beat time : it was generally the first movement of the 17th- and 18th-century dance suites.

ANDANTE (It.) : Walking pace.

ANDANTINO (It.) : Originally meant slower than andante, but as andante is now used to mean "slow", andantino means quicker than andante.

ANTHEM : A piece for church choir with or without

solos, sung during the Anglican church service, but not forming part of the liturgy ; also sung in other English-speaking Protestant churches.

ARABESQUE (Fr.) : A term used by Schumann and Debussy for pieces containing ornamental melodic figures—originally applied to Arabic and Moorish architectural ornamentation.

ARIA (It.) : A song or air usually in three sections, A, B, A. There are many such arias in 18th-century operas and oratorios. (See *Recitative*.)

AUBADE (Fr.) : A morning song generally sung by the lover under his lady's window.

AYRE (Old Eng.) : A 16th- to 17th-century song with melodic interest mostly in the top part—often applied to a solo song with lute accompaniment.

An Opera Singer

BADINAGE (Fr.)
BADINERIE (Fr.) } A light, playful type of 18th-century instrumental piece in quick two-beat time.

BAGATELLE (Fr.) : A short piece, usually—a mere trifle—humorous or light in character.

BALLAD OPERA : See *Opera*.

BALLADE (Fr.) : A romantic type of piano piece having a narrative quality. It was a term first used by Chopin to describe certain of his piano pieces.

BALLETT or BALLET (Old Eng.) : A 16th–17th-century choral piece similar to a madrigal, but lighter and more dance-like in rhythm; sometimes it was intended that the singers should dance.

BALLET MUSIC : Music for a stage entertainment consisting entirely of dancing.

BARCAROLLE (Fr.) : A song or piece in the style of a Gondolier's boat-song, as, for ex-

ample, Offenbach's *Barcarolle*.

BASSE DANSE (Fr.) : A 14th–16th-century French dance, in which the dancers' feet were kept low, hence its name, which means *a low dance.*

BASSO OSTINATO (It.) : Literally, *obstinate bass.* See *Ground Bass.*

BERGERETTE (Fr.) : A little shepherd song

123

—usually associated with 18th-century French artificiality.

BOLERO (Sp.): A lively Spanish dance with castanets, in three-beat time. (See *Seguidilla*.)

BOURRÉE (Fr.): Originally a French peasant dance in four-four time, with every phrase beginning on the fourth beat of a bar. It was often used as one of the livelier movements of a suite.

BRANLE (Fr.)
BRAWL (Eng.)

An old French dance: From the old French word *branler* —to swing from side to side.

The Bourrée

CACCIA (It.): Chase or hunt.

CACHUCHA (Sp.): An energetic solo Andalusian dance in three-beat time.

CADENZA (It.): A " showing-off " passage for (1) vocal display, introduced near the end of a song, (2) solo instrumental display in a concerto.

CANON : A piece of music consisting of one melody which, after having been begun in one voice or part, is continued in that part whilst it is begun in another, thus becoming interwoven with itself (canon, Two in One). A third voice (canon, Three in One), and more, may enter in the same way. The round *Three Blind Mice* is a form of canon.

CANTATA (It.) : A short secular or sacred work for solo voices or choir with orchestral accompaniment.

CANZONA (It.) : A part-song or instrumental piece in madrigal style, but lighter in character and simpler in construction.

CAPELLMEISTER (Ger.) : See *Kapellmeister*.

CAPRICCIO (It.) / CAPRICE (Fr.) : Usually applied to a short lively piece.

CAVATINA (It.) : A melody, sung or played, in the style of a simple short song.

CEBELL : An early English gavotte, rather quicker that the gavotte proper.

CHACONNE (Fr.) : Originally this was a slow three-in-a-bar dance, but it now consists of variations on a ground bass (which see).

CHAMBER MUSIC : A term applied to concerted music for from two to nine (or ten) players (or singers—more rarely), with one performer to each part.

A Chamber Music Trio

CHORAL (Ger.) ⎰ The traditional German Lutheran
CHORALE (Eng.) ⎱ hymn-tune.

CHORALE PRELUDE : A type of organ piece used in German churches in the 17th and 18th centuries to introduce and elaborate the hymn to be sung by the congregation.

CLASSICAL MUSIC : Music which has proved its worth. It usually means music composed between the 17th and early 19th century.

CLAVIER : See *Klavier*.

CODA (It.) : Literally, *tail*. A finishing passage or section at the end of a piece.

COMIC OPERA : See *Opera*.

CONCERT OVERTURE : See *Overture*.

CONCERTO (It.) : Literally, a performance in concert.

(1) *Concerto Grosso* (It.) : A work for two groups of instruments playing in concert and answering each other ; the larger group is called *ripieno* (full), and the smaller (often solo instruments) *concertino*.

(2) *Classical Concerto* : This is in the form of a symphony with the minuet movement omitted, for orchestra and a solo instrument, demanding brilliance and virtuosity from the soloist.

CONCERTSTUCK (Ger.) : See *Konzertstuck*.

CONSORT : An old English word meaning instruments playing together, such as a consort of viols. A *Broken Consort* signifies instruments of more than one type playing together. (Pl. 16.)

CONTINUO (It.) : *Figured Bass* or *Thorough Bass*.

A form of shorthand, whereby figures placed over or under a given bass show what harmony the composer desired to be filled in by the keyboard player. The given bass would be doubled by the lower strings.

CONTRAPUNTAL MUSIC : A term used for music made up of melodies combined in such a way that the resultant harmony is satisfying and the music is flowing (not progressing in blocks of chords).

CONTREDANSE (Fr.) : An English country dance, with the dancers facing each other.

COUNTERPOINT : The art of polyphonic composition. (See *Polyphony*.)

CZARDAS or CSARDAS : A Hungarian dance in two movements : slow, called *Lassu*, and quick, called *Friss*.

DIVERTIMENTO (It.)
DIVERTISSEMENT (Fr.) — (1) A light orchestral work (*a*) made up of a string of popular melodies, or (*b*) containing a number of contrasting movements similar to a suite, but longer. (2) In ballet, divertissement means a set of varied dances with no plot.

DIVISIONS : A 17th-century English term for variations.

DOUBLE : An old French name for divisions.

DUET, DUO : A composition for two voices or instruments with or without accompaniment, or for two players upon one instrument, as for example, in a piano duet.

DUMKA (Rus.): A Russian or Czech lament with alternating slow and animated sections. (*Dumky* = plural of *Dumka*.)

DUPLE TIME: Two-beat time.

ECOSSAISE (Fr.): A dance of Scottish origin. It is now applied to a lively piece in two-beat time of the country dance type.

ENTR'ACTE (Fr.): Originally meant any music played between parts of a play or a musical work. Later the name was applied to short concert pieces.

ÉTUDE (Fr.): Literally, *a study*. An instrumental exercise in technique and/or expression. Some études are written for public performance. (See *Chopin*, page 159.)

EXTEMPORISATION: The same as improvisation, which see.

FANCY: An old English name for a form of polyphonic chamber music. Fancies generally consisted of several correlated sections, performed without a break.

FANDANGO (Sp.): A lively Spanish dance in three-beat time, played by guitar and danced with castanets. There are intervals during which the dancers sing.

PL. 23.   *A One Man Percussion Band*
(*Percussion—*p. 102)

PL. 24.   *An early nineteenth century Military Drummer (The Bass Drum—p.* 105)

FANFARE : A trumpet
  flourish.
FANTASIA (It.) ⎫
FANTASIE (Fr.) ⎬
FANTASY (Eng.)⎭
  See *Fancy*. This can
  either mean a com-
  position based on
  themes from opera
  or folk-songs, or a
  composition based
  on popular tunes.
FARANDOLE (Fr.) : A
  Provençal proces-
  sional dance, in six-
  beat time, performed
  through the streets to the accompaniment of
  pipe and tabor. (See page 72.)
FIGURED BASS : See *Continuo*.
FIRST MOVEMENT FORM : See *Sonata Form*.
FOLÍA or FOLLIA (It.) : Originally this was a wild
  Portuguese dance. One particular tune was
  very popular among composers of the 17th
  and 18th centuries, who wrote many variations on it over a ground bass (which see).
FUGA (It.) ⎰ A polyphonic piece having a fixed
FUGUE (Fr.) ⎱ number of melodic strands or voices,
  comparable with the soprano, alto,
  tenor and bass of a choir. It is
  based on a short theme called a subject, which is introduced by each
  voice in turn. Each voice then con-
  tinues its own line in satisfactory

I   129

FUGA (It.)
FUGUE (Fr.)
—contd.

combination with the others until all voices have made one entry. After this " exposition " further entries of the original subject are made between freer passages, called " episodes ". Many ingenious modifications of the subject may be made, such as *Augmentation*—spacing it out in longer note values, or *Diminution*—squashing it into smaller note values, or *Inversion*—turning it upside down. Other devices used are *Stretto*—making the entries of the subject tumble in on each other more quickly, and *Pedal*—sustaining one note, usually the bass, during the progress of the other parts.

GAGLIARDA (It.)
GALLIARD (Fr.)

A lively three-beat-time dance, which was usually associated with the *Pavane*, which it followed and often contained the same music in different rhythm. Popular in the 15th and 16th centuries.

GALOP : A vigorous two-beat time round dance, popular early in the 19th century.

GAVOTTE : A four-beat time dance form, with

every phrase beginning on the third beat. Was often one of the lively movements of the suite. (Compare with the Bourrée.)

GIGA (It.)
GIGUE (Fr.) : A lively dance form in three-, six-, nine- or twelve-beat time, often appearing as one of the movements of the suite.

GLEE : A secular part-song intended to be sung by a choir. This type of song was very popular in 19th-century England. The melodic interest is in the top part, and the music is repeated for each verse.

GOPAK : A lively two-beat time Russian dance.

GRAND OPERA : An opera devoid of spoken dialogue. (See *Opera*.)

GRAVE : Solemn.

GRAZIOSO (It.) : Gracefully.

GREGORIAN CHANT : See *Plainsong*.

The Gopak

GROUND BASS : A bass which is repeated many times with variations built above it.

HABANERA (Sp.) : A slow dance from Cuba, which became popular in Spain. *Habanera* comes from the word *Havana*, the chief town of the Island.

HAMMERKLAVIER (Ger.) : Pianoforte. Literally, *hammer keyboard*.

HARMONY : The sounding together of musical

tones of varying pitch, which make sense to the musical ear.

HOPAK : See *Gopak*.

HORNPIPE : An old English dance in three-beat time ; later in two-beat time. Associated with sailors. It gets its name from the instrument which accompanied it.

HUMORESK or HUMORESQUE : A title given to a short instrumental piece, humorous or capricious in character. A well-known example is Dvorak's *Humoresque*.

IDYLL : A title given to a short instrumental piece of a quiet, fanciful or pastoral character. An example of this form is the *Siegfried Idyll* of Wagner.

IMPROMPTU (It.) : This word really means a short extemporised piece, but the title is applied to short compositions.

IMPROVISATION : Music composed while being performed. The name is also given to pieces which are free in style and sound as if improvised.

INCIDENTAL MUSIC : Any music performed during a spoken play, as, for example, Greig's incidental music to Ibsen's *Peer Gynt*.

INTERLUDE ⎫
⎬ (Fr.) See *Entr'acte*.
INTERMEDE ⎭

INTERMEZZO (It.): A short piano or orchestral piece. See also *Entr'acte*.

INTRADA (It.): See *Overture*.

INVENTION: J. S. Bach uses this title for a type of short contrapuntal keyboard piece. A short melodic phrase is announced, and a whole composition is developed or " invented " from it.

JAZZ: A type of popular music, originally coming from the United States about 1914 and owing much to negro influence, which has spread almost all over the world. The development of the use of saxophones, syncopation and unusual sound effects both in orchestration and chord progressions are some of its main features.

JIG (Eng.): See *Gigue*.

JOTA (Sp.): A rapid three-beat dance with castanets, from Northern Spain.

KAPELLMEISTER (Ger.): Master, or director of music in the establishment of a German prince, nobleman or high ecclesiastic, who was responsible for all the music in concert-room, opera-house and church. One of his duties was to compose for all court occasions.

KEY: (Readers should refer to plan of pianoforte keyboard given at the end of

133

the book.) A particular group of notes on which a composition is mainly centred forms its key. The most important note is the key-note, and the relationships of the other notes to this determine their character. There are two main types of key—Major and Minor. As an example, play from C to C on the white notes on a pianoforte : this constitutes the scale of C major, with the half-tones between the third and fourth notes (E and F) and the seventh and eighth (B and C). Play it again, but, instead of E, play E flat : the ascending form of C minor is heard, with the half-tones between the second and third and the seventh and eighth notes. The distance from C to E is greater than the distance from C to E flat— hence the terms major and minor. Similar scales can be built from any note, and the first note is always the key note ; the others constitute the notes of that key.

KEY-NOTE : See above.

KINDERSTUCK (Ger.) : Children's piece.

KLAVIER (Ger.) : Keyboard. It now signifies pianoforte; it used to mean harpsichord or clavichord. The organ keyboard is sometimes so called. See *The Well-tempered Klavier* (page 154).

KOCHEL : Dr. Ludwig Ritter Von, 1800–1877 : Austrian naturalist and learned musician. He compiled a systematic catalogue of Mozart's works (published in 1862, revised by Alfred Einstein in 1937). All Mozart's works are referred to by their Köchel number instead of by their opus number. (See *Opus*.)

KONZERTSTUCK (Ger.): A short type of concerto. Sometimes found as a title on piano music, meaning—for concert performance.

LANDLER: A German three-beat dance, from which the waltz developed.

LANGSAM (Ger.): Slow.

LARGO (It.): Slow and stately, as for example, Handel's *Largo*.

LEBHAFT (Ger.): Lively.

LEITMOTIV: A short theme associated with an idea, an object or a person in an opera, which appears and reappears at appropriate moments. The device used frequently by Wagner (see page 181), was used earlier by Mozart, Weber, Berlioz and others.

LENTO (It.): Slow.

LESSON: See *Suite*.

LIBRETTO: The word-part of an opera.

LIED (Ger.): Song. *Lieder ohne Worte*—song without words. (See *Mendelssohn*, page 169.)

MADRIGAL: A composition for several voices,

Madrigal Singers and Players

polyphonic (which see) in style, usually secular, and having words of high literary value, in the native language of the composer (and not in Latin, as had been the custom). It dates from the 14th century, but the late 16th and early 17th century was the period of the English madrigal. Madrigals could be played as well as sung (see also *Ayre* and *Ballett*).

MAESTOSO (It.) : Majestically.

MALE VOICE CHOIR
MALE VOICE QUARTET } There are usually four parts : one alto, two tenors and one bass ; there are many voices to each part in a choir, but only one to each in a quartet. The term can also apply to a choir or quartet of men and boys.

MARCIA, ALLA (It.)
MARCIA (It.)
MARZIALE (It.) }
In the style of a march.

MASCARADE : A Masked Ball, or music suggesting it. Originally it was the French equivalent of the English Masque.

MASQUE : A costly entertainment, indulged in by the nobility before opera was developed. Music, poetry, scenic effects, dancing and action were used in the productions of dramas based on some myth or allegory, as for example, Milton's *Comus*, for which Henry Lawes wrote the music.

MASS: The celebration of the Eucharist. A musical setting of it is also called Mass.

MAZURKA or MAZUR (Polish): A three-beat Polish national dance from the 16th century or earlier. The second beat tends to be accented. Chopin composed a number of piano pieces in this form.

MENO (It.): Less.

MENUET (Fr.)
MENUETTO (It.)
MINUET (Eng.)

A three-beat French country dance, which was adopted and modified by the court of Louis XIV towards the end of the 17th century, from whence it rapidly became popular throughout Europe. In this graceful modified form it was sometimes used in old suites, and it is frequently met with in the classical sonata. In the sonatas and symphonies of Haydn and later composers, the *menuetto* is often found, but its character has changed, becoming quicker and livelier, and in some of Beethoven's works it is often superseded by the scherzo. Often a second menuetto is present, termed trio (which see).

MIXED VOICES: A choir or an ensemble with soprano, alto, tenor and bass voices.

MODERATO : At a moderate speed.

MODULATION : A gradual change of key.

MOLTO (It.) : Much.

MOMENT MUSICAL : A title favoured by Schubert for some of his piano pieces ; a fanciful name for a short instrumental work.

MORGENLIED (Ger.) : See *Aubade*.

MOSSO (It.) : Movement (*Un poco*, a little ; *piu*, more ; *meno*, less).

MOTET : A church anthem, usually unaccompanied. Also applied now-a-days to a secular work of the same type.

MOTO (It.) : Motion. *Moto perpetuo*—perpetual motion.

MOUVEMENT PERPETUEL : See above.

MUSETTE (Fr.) : The name for French bagpipes (see page 81) : also applied to a dance with a drone-bass. Often a gavotte with a drone-bass in an old suite is so named, sandwiched between another gavotte and its repeat : *Gavotte, Musette, Gavotte.*

NACHT MUSIK (Ger.) : Literally, *night-music*—a piece of music for light evening entertainment.

NACHT STUCK (Ger.) : Literally, *night piece.*

NOCTURNE : Used by some composers to mean the same as *Serenade.* John Field, an Irish composer, adopted, and Chopin very much used, the title for a slow, romantic type of piano piece.

NONET : A work for nine performers.

NOTTURNO (It.) : See *Nocturne.*

NOVELETTE : Used by Schumann and borrowed by others as a title for short piano pieces of romantic nature. Literally, *a short story.*

OBBLIGATO (It.)
OBLIGATO
(The first is the correct spelling.) A solo instrumental part, which is of outstanding importance in a work, is said to be an obbligato, i.e. compulsory or obligatory.

OCTET : A work for eight performers.

OPENING SYMPHONY : A term sometimes given to the opening instrumental bars of a song.

OPERA (It.) : A sung play with orchestra.

OPERA, BALLAD (Eng.) : A light, farcical English opera, often parodying the Grand Opera. The first ballad opera was *The Beggar's Opera*, which was followed by many others in the course of the 18th century. Vaughan Williams has called *Hugh the Drover* a ballad opera, although apart from the simplicity of language and theme, it has little in common with the earlier kind of ballad opera.

Polly, in The Beggar's Opera

OPERA, BUFFA (It.)
OPERA, BUFFE (Fr.)
OPERA, COMIC
Opera on a comic subject, usually with spoken dialogue.

OPERA COMIQUE (Fr.) : A term used by the French

to include most operas with spoken dialogue (as opposed to Grand Opera), and should not be confused with Comic Opera, for the subject can be semi-tragic, as in *Don Giovanni*.

OPERA, GRAND : Opera without spoken dialogue.

OPUS (Latin) : Literally, *work*. Since the 18th century composers have labelled their compositions in consecutive order—thus *Opus* 1 would signify an early work, and *Opus* 101 a much later one. Unfortunately, some composers have not been very accurate in this matter. *Op. Post.* (*Opus posthumous*) is a work published after the composer's death. (See *Köchel*.)

ORATORIO (It.) : A sacred opera without action. Handel used the term also for secular works.

ORDRE (Fr.) : See *Suite*.

OSTINATO or BASSO OSTINATO (It.) : Literally, *an obstinate bass*. (See *Ground Bass*.)

OVERTURE : An opening piece for an opera, an oratorio, an instrumental suite, or a play.

CONCERT OVERTURE : Sometimes such an overture would be played at a concert, being severed from the work to which it originally belonged, e.g. Mendelssohn's *Overture to a Midsummer Night's Dream*. Owing to the popularity of the overture as a form of composition, composers in modern times have written orchestral works, calling them overtures, although they have no connection with any larger work. Mendelssohn's *Hebrides* is an example of this kind of overture.

PARTITA (It.) : See *Suite*.

PART SONG : A vocal piece for several voices, with
or without accompaniment, particularly popular in 19th century.

PASSACAGLIA (It.) ⎱ The same as the chaconne
PASSACAILLE (Fr.) ⎰ (which see).

PASSEPIED (Fr.) : A dance similar to a minuet.

PASSION MUSIC : The story of Christ's Passion set
to music vocally with solo voices, chorus and
orchestra.

PASTORAL : A rustic piece, often associated with the

shepherd's pipe or the bagpipes, sometimes
with an appropriate drone bass. The quiet
pastoral atmosphere is maintained in the six-
beat or twelve-beat in a bar rhythm. An
example of this form is Bach's *Pastorale* in *The*

Christmas Oratorio. The pastoral has much the same form as the siciliana (which see).

PAVANE or PAVAN : A slow (two-beat) stately dance popular in the 16th century. It was usually followed by the Galliard. A modern work, based on the Pavane, is Ravel's *Pavane for a Dead Infanta.*

PERPETUUM MOBILE : See *Moto.*

PHANTASY : A term used in the 20th century for a piece of string chamber-music in one movement, with no set forms.

PHRASE : A small group of notes, more or less complete in itself, very often lasting for two or four bars. A number of phrases make a sentence. The phrase in music can be said to be analogous to the sentence in the literary sense, and the musical sentence to the paragraph.

PIANO QUARTET : A sonata for piano and three " strings."

PIANO QUINTET : A sonata for piano and four " strings."

PIANO TRIO : A sonata for piano and two " strings."

PIPE and TABOR : A three-holed " whistle " flute and a small drum, both performed together by one player. (See page 72.)

PIU (It.) : More.

PLAINSONG : Ancient traditional unison song, still used, of the Christian Church. Plainsong chanting is sometimes called Gregorian, after Pope Gregory (590–604), who formulated rules on which it is based.

POLKA : A lively dance from Bohemia (in two-beat time), danced in couples. It originated in the early 19th century. Smetana introduced a polka into his opera *The Bartered Bride*.

POLYPHONY : A number of melodic strands which are woven together to make musical sense.

POSTLUDE : A piece played after a ceremony.

PRAELUDIUM : A Prelude (see *Overture*). Often a piece which preceded an instrumental fugue. Also a title for a short instrumental piece.

PRESTISSIMO (It.) : Very quick.

PRESTO (It.) : Quick.

PROGRAMME MUSIC : Music which " tells a story " in sound. This type of music became popular in the 19th century.

QUADRUPLE TIME : Four-beat time.

QUARTET : A piece for four performers.

QUINTET : A piece for five performers.

RECITATIVE
RECITATIVO (It.) } Song declamation, with fixed notes, but indefinite time. Often used to provide the connecting narrative link between the arias in an opera, and similarly in an oratorio.

REQUIEM : A mass for the dead.

RHAPSODY : An ecstatic type of instrumental composition, first popularised by Liszt.

RIGADOON (Eng.)
RIGAUDON (Fr.) } An old Provençal dance in two-beat or four-beat time.

RIPIENO (It.) : See *Concerto*.

RITORNELLO (It.) : An instrumental passage in a vocal composition (when the voice is silent).

ROMANCE (1) (Eng.) : A short song-like instrumental piece.

(2) (Fr.) : A song.

ROMANTIC MUSIC : Music with strong romantic feeling, composed mostly during the first half of the 19th century. Comparable, and almost contemporary with the Romantic Schools of Literature and Painting.

ROMANZA (It.) : See *Romance* (1).

RONDEAU (Fr.) : A piece in which the main tune appears at least three times, interspersed between other " episodes " as the contrasting sections are called.

RONDINO (It.) : A short piece in the form of a Rondo.

RONDO (It.) : See *Rondeau*.

RUBATO—TEMPO RUBATO (It.) : " Robbed time ". For purposes of expression in some compositions the performer hurries over some

PL. 25. *The Serpent* (p. 100)

PL. 26. Top Left, *A Portable Organ*. Top Right, *A Bible Regal*. Below, *A Positive Organ* (p. 117)

notes, and lingers over others thus robbing some to pay the others.

RUHIG (Ger.): Peacefully.

SALTARELLO (It.): See *Galliard*.

SARABANDE (Fr.): This was originally a slow solo court dance. It is in three-beat time, with the accent frequently coming on the second beat. The form is found in 17th- and 18th-century suites.

SCALE: A "ladder". Notes of a key arranged in order, such as C major: C D E F G A B C. See also *Key*.

SCHERZO (It.): A "joke". Often a humorous type of movement which has replaced the minuet (which see) in the sonata and symphony.

SCHNELL (Ger.): Quick.

SCORE: A full copy of the music—as distinct from a "part", in which the individual performer has only his own part written.

FULL SCORE: A score showing all the parts of a vocal and orchestral work.

ORCHESTRAL SCORE: A music copy showing all the instrumental parts of an orchestral work.

VOCAL SCORE: A music copy of a choral work giving all the voice-parts over a piano arrangement of the orchestral accompaniment.

K   145

SEGUIDILLA (Sp.) : An old Spanish dance in quick three-beat time. This dance has an ancient history, and was probably introduced into Spain by the Moors. The seguidilla has much in common with the bolero, but it is much faster. A feature of the dance are the sung passages within it, which are called *coplas*. Castanets are always used. Every province has its own form for this dance, but that of Andalusia is especially famous. Albeniz (see page 153) has made use of it in his piano compositions.

A Spanish Dancer of the Seguidilla with Castanets

SENTENCE : See *Phrase*.

SEPTET : A composition for seven performers.

SERENADE
SERENATA (It.) } An evening song generally sung by a lover under his lady's window. (Compare *Aubade*.)

SESTETTO : See *Sextet*.

SEVILLANA : A local type of seguidilla (which see).

SEXTET : A composition for six performers.

SICILIANA (It.)
SICILIANO (It.)
SICILIENNE (Fr.) } A Sicilian pastoral dance, in six-beat time. This form is found in sonatas and suites.

SINFONIA (Symphony) : In the 18th century it meant either an overture, out of which the music to a climax in readiness for the third section.

(3) *The Recapitulation*, in which there is a re-statement of the two subjects from (1), the second subject being in the same key as the opening of the movement. The Coda (a larger tail), in contrast to the Codetta (a little tail), which has come earlier, finishes the movement.

When a movement is said to be in a certain key (say Sonata in C), it means that it begins and ends in that key, and most likely the second subject in (1) would be in G.

Sonatina (It.): A work shorter and simpler than a Sonata.

Song without Words: A title used by Mendelssohn for a number of his short piano pieces.

Sostenuto (It.): Sustained.

Standchen (Ger.): See *Serenade*.

Streichorchester (Ger.): String Orchestra.

STRING QUARTET : First and Second Violins, Viola and Violoncello.

STRING TRIO : Three string instruments. [Note.—Many works for String Quartet, Piano Trio, String Trio, etc. (Chamber music) are in Sonata form, which see].

SUBJECT : A theme—see *Fugue*, also *Sonata Form.*

SUITE, ORDRE (Fr.)
PARTITA (It.)
LESSON (Eng.)
{ An instrumental work, made up of a number of pieces to be played in succession. The early 18th-century suite usually consisted of pieces in the following dance forms : *allemande, courante, sarabande* and *gigue.* Sometimes it opened with a prelude, and other dances, such as gavottes and bourrées, were included after the sarabande. The title Suite is also applied to modern works consisting of various movements but lacking the formality of sonata structure.

SYMPHONIC POEM : A large work for orchestra in one movement having a " programme ". A type of Romantic music introduced by Liszt.

SYMPHONIC VARIATIONS : Theme and variations for orchestra—a large type of composition—sometimes also requiring an instrumental soloist.

SYMPHONY (Classical) : (1) Literally it means "sounding together", and the word has been

used at different periods in different ways—
e.g. the overture was sometimes so called, as
was also the instrumental introduction to a
song.

(2) A work in sonata form (which see) for
Orchestra.

TARANTELLA (It.)
TARANTELLE (Fr.)
A quick dance in
six-beat time. It
was supposed to
be a cure for
Tarantism, a dis-
ease caused by
the bite of the
spider, Tarantula,
found round Ta-
ranto, in Italy.

TEMPO (It.) : Time.
TEMPO GIUSTO (It.) :
Strict time.

TEMPO RUBATO (It.) : See *Rubato*.

TERNARY FORM : See *Aria*. Three-fold form.

TERZETTO (It.) : A piece for three performers
(Trio).

THEME : Air, melody or subject of a piece of music.

THOROUGH BASS : see *Continuo*.

TOCCATA (It.) : A "touch piece". A title given to
rapid and brilliant keyboard pieces.

TONE POEM : Symphonic Poem (which see).

TORDION (Fr.) : An old Basque dance in three-
beat time.

TRANSPOSING INSTRUMENTS : To simplify the

technical difficulties involved in the performance of some instruments, the music is not written in the key in which it is intended to sound. The clarinet player in an orchestra has two instruments; one in B flat and the other in A. When he sees the note C written in his music, he associates that note with a certain fingering, which, when used on the B-flat instrument, produces the note B flat, and on the A instrument produces the note A. If, therefore, the composer wishes the player to *sound* the note C on the B flat instrument, he must write the note D (a whole tone higher than it sounds, because the note produced will sound a whole tone lower). Similarly, for the A instrument to sound C he must write the note E flat (a tone and a half higher than it sounds, because the note produced will sound a tone and a half lower). Horns, trumpets and clarinets are the chief transposing instruments. (See pages 184–5.)

TREPAK: A Russian dance similar to the Gopak.

TRIO (It.): (1) A work for three performers.

(2) Sometimes a second minuet, or a second scherzo in the later symphonies between the first and second part of the minuet or scherzo. Sometimes these movements were written in three-part harmony, hence the name.

TRIPLE TIME: Three-beat time.

TRIPLET: Three notes played in the time of two.

TUTTI (It.): "Everyone" in contrast to (1) *Solo* in a concerto, or to (2) *Divisi*, when one string section in an orchestra plays more than one part instead of normally playing in unison.

UN POCO (It.) : A little.

VARIATIONS : Varied treatments of a given theme. See *Air and Variations*.

VIVACE, VIVO (It.) : Lively.

VORSPIEL (Ger.) : Overture or Prelude.

WIEGENLIED (Ger.) : Cradle-song.

ZAPATEADO (Sp.) : A fierce Spanish dance in three-beat time, accompanied with stamping instead of castanets.

ZIGEUNERLIED (Ger.) : Gipsy song.

ZINGARA, ALLA (It.) : In Gipsy style.

PART FOUR

Composers

CHAPTER VII

BIOGRAPHICAL NOTES

ALBENIZ, ISAAC (1860–1909). Spanish pianist and composer for the piano. One of the first Spanish composers to exploit native idioms. In Paris he came under the influence of Dukas and Debussy. *Works include*: operas, *The Magic Opal, Henry Clifford*; piano works, *Catalonia, La Vega, Iberia* (cycle of twelve), etc.

ARENSKY, ANTONY (1861–1906). Professor at Moscow Conservatorium 1882, Director of Music in the Imperial Chapel at St. Petersburg, 1894. Wrote numerous works in which he made much use of folk tunes.

ARNE, THOMAS (1710–1778). The leading British composer of his day. He is chiefly remembered for his songs, particularly *Rule Britannia*. *Works include*: operas, *Tom Thumb the Great*, etc.; instrumental music, including incidental music to many of Shakespeare's plays; twenty-five books of songs.

ARNOLD, MALCOLM (1921–   ). English composer and trumpet player. He has written orchestral, chamber, and incidental music.

BACH (the Family). There were generations of musicians, the most important of the group being:

BACH, JOHANN SEBASTIAN (1685–1750), considered one of the greatest composers. Born in North Germany, when music was of great importance in court life, religious observances and municipal functions. Supreme organist of his day. Work  falls into three sections, corresponding to the different posts he held: (*a*) organ works, (*b*) orchestral and other compositions, (*c*) church compositions. *Works include: Passions of St. John*, and *St. Matthew, Mass in B Minor*; over two hundred church cantatas. *The Well-tempered Klavier* (forty-eight preludes and fugues), numerous organ works, etc., six *Brandenburg Concertos*.

BACH, C. P. E. (1714–1788). Johann Sebastian Bach's second son. He was the chief founder of the sonata-symphony style, later developed by Haydn, Mozart and Beethoven.

BACH, J. C. (1735–1782). Johann Sebastian Bach's youngest son. Spent much of his life as opera and concert director in London and was appointed music master to George III, hence he is known as the " The English Bach ".

BALAKIREF, MILY (1837–1910). Did much to encourage young Russian composers, founder of a group called " The Five ". Edited Russian folk-tunes, although much of his own music is " oriental " rather than Russian in feeling. His piano music shows the influence of Liszt. *Works include:* two symphonies; symphonic poem, *Thamar*; piano-pieces and songs.

BARBER, SAMUEL (1910–   ). American composer of ballet, choral, orchestral, military and chamber music, also songs.

BARTÓK, BÉLA (1881–1945). Born in Hungary, died in New York. His early style influenced by

Brahms and Dohnanyi. Through his study (with Kodály) of ancient Magyar tunes with their strange harmonies, he developed new harmonies in his own work. The strangeness of his compositions aroused opposition. *Works include:* concertos, orchestral works, operas, quartets, much piano-music.

BATESON, THOMAS (1570–1630). English composer of madrigals. Ended his life as vicar choral and organist at Trinity Cathedral, Dublin.

BAX, ARNOLD (1883–1953). Born in London, and knighted 1937. Master of the King's Musick, 1942. Much of his work shows Celtic influence. A prolific composer. *Works include: The Garden of Fand; Tintagel; Symphonic Variations* and other orchestral pieces; music for ballet; chamber and piano music.

BEETHOVEN, LUDWIG VAN (1770–1827), is considered one of the greatest composers. In early life he had some teaching from Mozart, Haydn and others, and then settled in Vienna. He composed slowly, and with effort. He is sometimes called the last of the classical composers and the first of the romantics; his work is a development  of that of Mozart and an inspiration for that of Wagner. *Works include:* nine symphonies, overtures; seventeen string quartets; thirty-two pianoforte sonatas; *Mass in D;* The opera, *Fidelio;* concertos, etc.

BELLINI, VINCENZO (1801–1835). Born in Sicily. Popular composer of operas, who gave the singer every opportunity to display charm and technical ability. Chopin admired his flowing melodies. *Operatic works include: Zaira, Norma, I Puritani.*

BERG, ALBAN (1885–1935). Born in Vienna. A disciple of Schoënberg, and composer of *Wozzeck*. *Lulu*, another opera, was unfinished at his death; also wrote chamber and some orchestral music.

BERKELEY, LENNOX (1903–). Born near Oxford, partly of French descent, and has studied in France. One of the most skilled of modern British composers—and unafraid of harmonic innovation and directness. Has written numerous works, including an oratorio, *Jonah*, and ballet music, chamber music, piano music and some choral works.

BERLIOZ, HECTOR (1803–1869). The greatest figure in the French romantic movement. The value of his work is constantly debated, much being grandiose; his work is orchestrally colourful. Introduced the idea of a recurring theme which varies in treatment according to the context (idée fixe). *Works include: operas, Beatrice and Benedict, Les Troyens,* etc.; " programme " symphonies, including *Symphonie fantastique* and *Harold in Italy*; twenty-five choral works, including *La Damnation de Faust, Messe des Morts.*

BERNERS, LORD GERALD (1883–1950). Born at Bridgnorth, and entered the diplomatic service. Was for a short time a pupil of Stravinsky. Some of his works show a sense of humour and have the quality of parody. *Works include:* a one act opera; ballets, etc.

BIZET, GEORGES (1838–1875). A French composer, whose most successful work, *Carmen*, was produced only a few months before his death; his other operas were less successful. *Works include:*

operas, *The Pearl-fishers*, *The Fair Maid of Perth*; incidental music to Daudet's play *L'Arlesienne*, which is often heard as two orchestral suites.

BLISS, ARTHUR (1891–). Studied at Cambridge and at the Royal College of Music. Musical Director, B.B.C. 1941–1944. Master of the Queen's Musick, 1954. Work independent in character; frequently composes for unusual combinations of instruments. *Works include: Colour Symphony*; the ballet *Checkmate*; music to the H. G. Wells' film *The Shape of Things to Come*.

BLOCH, ERNEST (1880–1959). Born in Switzerland of Jewish parents. Often used Jewish themes in his compositions. He became an American citizen. Many of his works have been first performed in the U.S.A. *Works include:* opera, *Macbeth*; *Sacred Service* (*Avodath Hakdesh*); *Israel Symphony for Five Voices and Orchestra*. A society was formed in London in 1937 to secure performance of his works.

BORODIN, ALEXANDER (1833–1887). A Russian composer, also a professor of chemistry and a medical man who founded a School of Medicine for Women. He was one of the "Five", the others being Balakiref, Cui, Mussorgsky and Rimsky-Korsakof. All these were amateur musicians who earned their living in other professions. *Works include:* two symphonies; opera, *Prince Igor*; three string quartets.

BRAHMS, JOHANNES (1833–1897). Born in Hamburg. Germany's outstanding classic-romantic composer. He was helped by Joachim and Liszt,

and formed a life-long friendship with Schumann and his wife. Last thirty-five years of his life were spent in Vienna. *Works include :* four symphonies ; a violin concerto ; a violin and 'cello concerto ; two piano concertos ; choral-orchestral compositions, e.g. *German Requiem* ; overtures, *Academic Festival Overture*, etc.

BRITTEN, BENJAMIN (1913–). Born in Lowestoft. Has studied under Frank Bridge, John Ireland and Arthur Benjamin. Has a technical assurance and style owing little to his immediate English predecessors. Britten has produced a large number of first-rate works. *Works include :* songs, *Seven Sonnets of Michael Angelo*, etc. ; *Spring Symphony* ; operas, *Peter Grimes*, *Albert Herring*, *The Rape of Lucretia*, *Billy Budd*, *Let's Make an Opera* ; *Gloriana* ; *The Young Person's Guide to the Orchestra*.

BRUCKNER, ANTON (1824–1896). Born in Upper Austria, and composed many large-scale works. Influenced by Wagner. There is a certain naivety in his work, and it is not popular outside Germany and Austria.

BULL, JOHN (1563–1628). An English composer of anthems, secular choral works, numerous pieces for virginals and the organ.

BUSONI, FERRUCCIO (1866–1924). Of half-Italian, half-German parentage. His later

158

works are anti-romantic in character. Orchestral and chamber music. Three operas, including *Turandot*.

BYRD, WILLIAM (1543–1623). Born probably in Lincoln, a pupil and later a friend of Tallis. Joint organist with Tallis of Queen Elizabeth's Chapel Royal. Composer of fine church music, madrigals and keyboard music. Father of English music.

CARPENTER, JOHN A. (1876–1951). American business man who gained popularity as composer of orchestral works, piano pieces, etc.

CHAUSSON, ERNEST (1855–1899). Born in Paris, and trained for the law. Became a pupil of Massenet, and then joined the César Franck circle. Compositions show influence of Franck, Wagner and Brahms.

CHOPIN, FREDERICK (1810–1849). Born in Poland of half-Polish, half-French parentage, he spent much of his life in Paris. A romantic, personal composer, who has enormously increased the pianist's repertoire. Died of consumption. *Works include :* twenty-seven études, twenty-five preludes, nineteen nocturnes, fifty-two mazurkas, and two concertos.

COLERIDGE-TAYLOR, SAMUEL (1875–1912). Son of an English woman and of a West African negro medical student. Brought a new and personal idiom into British music. *Works include :*

Hiawatha's Wedding Feast; *African Suite*; works for orchestra, chamber music and incidental music for plays.

COPLAND, AARON (1900–). Born in U.S.A., prolific composer of the more popular types of orchestral and chamber music, sometimes showing Jewish and jazz influence.

COUPERIN, FRANÇOIS (1668–1733). Sometimes known as " Couperin le Grand ", to distinguish him from his other musical relations. At twenty-five he became organist of Louis XIV's chapel at Versailles. Today chiefly known for his delicate harpsichord music. He was an early writer of " Programme Music " (see page 143).

CUI, CESAR (1835–1918). Born at Vilna, a Russian of French origin. Became a general in the Russian army. Wrote a number of works, none of them distinctively national in tone. He was one of the " Five " (see Borodin).

DEBUSSY, CLAUDE (1862–1918). French composer who was, from the age of twelve, a student at the Paris Conservatoire. His music has a delicate suggestiveness, rather than the firm statement— and this allies him with the impressionist painters of his day. *Works include*: opera, *Pelléas et Mélisande*; incidental music, *Le martyre de saint Sebastian*, etc.; *Prelude à l'après-midi d'un faune*, and numerous piano pieces.

DELIBES, LÉO (1836–1891). French composer of light, delightful ballet music. *Works include*: ballets, *Coppelia*, *Sylvia*; opera, *Lakmé*; incidental music to Hugo's *Le Roi s'amuse*.

PL. 27. *A Cluster of Ancient Stringed Instruments*

Pl. 28. *Ancient Instruments*

DELIUS, FREDERICK (1862–1934). Born in Yorkshire of German parents. Grew oranges in Florida, then returned to Europe and taught the piano in Leipzig. A romantic of the impressionist school (see Debussy), with very individual harmony. Beecham made his work known in England. *Works include :* orchestral variations ; concertos ; choral-orchestral pieces ; operas, *A Village Romeo and Juliet*, etc.

DOHNÁNYI, ERNO (1877–1960). Born in Bratislava, became Musical Director to the Hungarian State Radio. A classical-romantic (see Brahms) ; composer of instrumental (especially chamber) music, and of piano pieces. A fine pianist.

DONIZETTI, GAETANO (1797–1848). An Italian operatic composer with a flair for melody, giving singers full opportunity to display their skill. *Work includes* over sixty operas, including : *Don Pasquale* ; *Elisir d'Amore* ; *Fille du Regiment* ; *Lucia di Lammermoor*.

DOWLAND, JOHN (1563–1620). Born probably in London. Greatest lute-player of the age, holding position as lutenist to the King of Denmark and to Charles I. Wrote delightful songs with lute and viol accompaniment. *Works include : Lachrymae* (three volumes of songs), *A Pilgrim's Solace*, etc.

DUKAS, PAUL (1865–1935). Born in Paris. Influenced by Lalo. When middle-aged burnt all his unpublished work and gave up composing. *Works include :* a symphonic scherzo, the *Prentice Sorcerer* ; the opera, *Ariadne and Bluebeard*.

DVOŘÁK, ANTONIN (1841–1904). Born near Prague. Studied music in poverty. Encouraged by Brahms. Features of his work are fresh and vigorous

orchestration. Influenced by
Bohemian and, to a lesser
extent, negro, idiom. *Works
include :* nine symphonies,
five symphonic poems ;
three *Slavonic Rhapsodies* ;
Scherzo Capriccioso ; *Stabat
Mater* ; *Humoresque* ; *Songs
my Mother Taught Me,*
etc.

DYSON, GEORGE (1883–1964). Born in Yorkshire.
Knighted 1941. He spent some time in Italy and
Germany. Produced large-scale choral works
and chamber music ; also a symphony and a violin
concerto. Director of Royal College of Music,
1937–1952.

ELGAR, SIR EDWARD (1857–
1934). Born in Worcester. Son
of an organist, and long a
violinist and teacher himself.
A typically British composer,
with a plain style and first-rate
orchestration. Less popular in
foreign countries. *Works include : Enigma Variations* ;
The Dream of Gerontius ; *Falstaff*,
etc. ; two symphonies ; concert overtures, including *Cockaigne*, a violin concerto and a 'cello concerto, and miscellaneous orchestral works.

FALLA, MANUEL DE (1876–1946). Born in Cadiz,
Spain, died in the Argentine. Lived for some
time in Paris, where he knew Debussy, Ravel and
Dukas. Wrote ballet music, and lighter orchestral
pieces. Influenced by Spanish folk idiom. *Works
include :* ballets, *The Three-Cornered Hat*, *Love*

the Magician; orchestral work, *Nights in the Gardens of Spain*, etc.

FAURE, GABRIEL (1845–1924). Director of Paris Conservatoire, 1905–1920, where he taught Nadia Boulanger, Grovlez, Ravel and Florent Schmitt. A prolific composer. His work is flowing, logical and finished. *Works include: Pelléas et Mélisande*; *Pavane*; eleven religious vocal pieces; ninety-six songs, including *Melodies de Verlaine*.

FERRARI, GUSTAVE (1872–1948). Born in Switzerland. A conductor, pianist, critic. Wrote songs and arranged folk-songs, etc.

FRANCK, CESAR (1822–1890).  Born in Liège. His first real success came just before his death at the age of sixty-eight, with the performance of his string quartet. Work romantic, with strong personal idiom, sometimes limited in scope. He was the leader of the heavy 19th-century romantic French School. *Works include : Symphonic Variations*; one symphony; works for choir and orchestra; masses; sixteen works for piano, nine for organ.

GATTY, NICHOLAS (1874–1946). Born in Sheffield. Critic and composer of operas. Had considerable stage sense. *Works include : Duke or Devil*; *Prince Ferelon*; *The Tempest*.

GIBBONS, ORLANDO (1583–1625). Born in Oxford. Finest keyboard player of his day, and organist to Westminster Abbey. A great name in the history of English church music, besides composing madrigals, music for viols, etc.

GLAZUNOV, ALEXANDER (1865–1936). Born in St. Petersburg. In early years a nationalist composer. At one time director of the St. Petersburg Conservatory, and honoured by the Soviet. Left Russia and settled in France. *Works include :* eight symphonies, piano, and violin concertos, ballet music, *Carnival*, etc.

GLINKA, MICHAEL (1804–1857). Born in the province of Smolensk, and brought up on his father's estate, where he heard much Russian folk-music. He is the father of the Russian national school of composers, and one of the founders of the romantic movement. *Russlan and Ludmilla,* his second opera, shows the influence of folk-music and also of " oriental " feeling, later found in much of Russian music.

GLUCK, CHRISTOPH (1714–1787). Born in Bavaria, died in Vienna. His operas, with rare exceptions, are the earliest still being performed. He reformed the stilted Italian operatic forms while in Paris, and his operas thus gained dramatic power. He wrote beautiful, pure music. *Works include : Orpheus and Eurydice, Alcestis,* etc.

GOOSSENS, EUGENE III (1893–1958). Born in London, one of a musical family. Spent much of his life in the U.S.A. Became Director of the Conservatory of New South Wales in 1947. Compositions include two operas.

GOUNOD, CHARLES (1818–1893). Born in Paris. A colourful, sentimental composer, given to over-sweetness, but had a lyrical and dramatic sense. *Works include :* operas, *Sapho, Faust, Romeo and Juliet* ; religious works.

GRANADOS, ENRIQUE (1867–1916). Born in Catalonia, Spain. He and his wife lost their lives when their ship was sunk by a submarine in the 1914–1918 war. Wrote piano music, using typically Spanish idioms, and miscellaneous orchestral works. *Works include :* operas, *Maria del Carmen*, *Goyescas* (based on a piano work) ; a *Symphonic Poem*, and suites for orchestra ; twelve *Spanish Dances*, etc.

GRIEG, EDWARD (1843–1907). A Norwegian composer, much of whose work reflects the spirit of his native land. Composer of smaller instrumental works, and fine, easy piano pieces. Wrote no symphonies or operas. *Works include :* incidental music, *Peer Gynt* ; piano concerto ; *Holberg Suite* ; one hundred and forty-three songs ; ten volumes of lyric piano pieces.

HANDEL, GEORGE F. (1685–1759). Born in Halle, in the same year as Bach. Studied in Italy, where he acquired his flowing style. Settled in England under patronage of George I. Composed for the large audience. *Works include :* oratorios, *Israel in Egypt*, *Messiah*, *Samson*, *Judas Maccabaeus* ; operas, *Berenice*, etc. ; twelve *Concerti Grossi*, and miscellaneous orchestral works ; *Water Music*.

HAYDN, JOSEPH (1732–1809). Born in Lower Austria. His works are based on the style of C. P. E. Bach, i.e. new sonata and symphony form. Numerous varied works, which include: over one hundred symphonies, the finest being the *Salomon Symphonies*; oratorios, *The Creation*, etc.

HINDEMITH, PAUL (1895–1963). Born in Germany. Performance of his work was forbidden by the Nazis. His output is large and modern, and varied in style. Has composed much for the violin and viola. *Works include:* operas, *Mathis der Maler*; symphonies.

HOLST, GUSTAV (1874–1934). Born in Cheltenham, of part Swedish parentage, one of a musical family. Began career as trombonist, then became Director of Music at St. Paul's Girls' School, Hammersmith. Music master at James Allen's Girls' School, Dulwich, and was connected with Morley College, Lambeth. All compositions highly original. *Work includes:* operas, *Savitri*, *The Perfect Fool*, *At the Boar's Head*; choral works, *Hymn of Jesus*; orchestral music, *The Planets*; folk-song arrangements.

HONEGGER, ARTHUR (1892–1955). A Swiss composer trained in Zurich and Paris. *Works include:* chamber music, orchestral music; operas, *Judith*, *Le roi David*; music for films.

HOPKINS, ANTONY (1921–). An English composer who has written sonatas, orchestral and choral works and Intimate Opera. Has done work also for radio, stage, ballet and films.

HOWELLS, HERBERT (1892–). Born in Gloucestershire. Professor at the Royal College of Music; succeeded Holst as Director of Music at St. Paul's Girls' School. Has composed orchestral works and organ music.

HUMPERDINCK, ENGELBERT (1854–1921). Born near Bonn. Friend of Wagner. *Chief work : Hansel and Gretel.*

IRELAND, JOHN (1879–1962). Born in Cheshire. Composed attractive songs, delicate music for the piano, and miscellaneous orchestral and choral works.

JANÁČEK, LEOŠ (1854–1928). Born in what is now Czechoslovakia. Composed various works, always of a strong national folk type. *Works include :* operas, *Jenufa, Kata Kabanova, Sarka* ; numerous choral works.

KODÁLY, ZOLTAN (1882–1967). Born in Hungary. Music national in spirit, and modern in tone. A friend of Bartok, and together they collected Hungarian folk tunes. *Works include :* plays with music, *Háry János* ; ballet music ; variations for orchestra ; piano works ; large number of songs, and choral works with and without orchestra.

LALO, EDOUARD (1823–1892). Born in Lille. Fine orchestrator. Had difficulty in arousing interest in his work. *Namouna*, a ballet, and his masterpiece, influenced Debussy and d'Indy. *Works include : Symphonie espagnole ; Roi d' Ys.*

LAMBERT, CONSTANT (1905–1951). Born in London, a pupil of Vaughan Williams. Conductor and composer, music critic, author. *Works in-*

clude : ballets, *Romeo and Juliet*, etc. ; *Summer's Last Will and Testament.*

LASSUS, ORLANDUS (1532–1594). Great Flemish composer of the high polyphonic period. His contemporaries were Byrd and Palestrina. Composed fine choral music.

LEONCAVALLO, RUGGIERO (1858–1919). Born in Naples. Earned his living for many years playing in cafés. His opera *I Pagliacci* (1892) brought him renown, nothing else he wrote meeting real success.

LISZT, FRANZ (1811–1886). Born in Hungary. Pianist prodigy. Champion of Wagner. When fifty, took orders and was known as Abbé Liszt, and composed Church music. Greater pianist than composer, and inspiring teacher. Invented the Symphonic Poem. *Works include :* four hundred piano pieces, nine hundred transcriptions for the piano ; twenty Hungarian Rhapsodies ; fourteen symphonic poems for orchestra.

LOEILLET, JEAN-BAPTISTE (1680–1730). Born in Ghent, and settled in London. Composer for the flute, clavichord, etc.

LULLY, JEAN-BAPTISTE (1632–1687). Born in Florence, brought up in France. Entered the service of Louis XIV, when he associated with Molière, and prepared music for ballets, masques and operas. He is famed for his fine handling of recitative in opera. Influenced Purcell.

LUTYENS, ELIZABETH (1906–   ). Born in London. Studied at Royal College of Music, and has composed miscellaneous works. Widow of the conductor Edward Clark, daughter of the architect.

MACONCHY, ELIZABETH (1907–). Born in Hertfordshire, and studied at the Royal College of Music, later at Prague. *Works include* a fine piano concerto, a *Comedy Overture*, and chamber music.

MAHLER, GUSTAV (1860–1911). Born in Bohemia. Jewish by race, Roman Catholic by conversion. A classical-romantic composer, influenced by Bruckner and Wagner. More highly regarded in Holland and Germany than elsewhere. *Works include :* ten symphonies, some with vocal parts ; song cycles, etc.

MASCAGNI, PIETRO (1863–1945). Born in Leghorn. A minor operatic conductor and piano teacher. His fame rests on *Cavalleria Rusticana*, produced when he was forty. Other operas followed, but achieved little success.

MASSENET, JULES (1842–1912). French composer of melodious operas, also orchestral works. *Works include : Manon, Thaïs, Sapho* ; oratorios ; thirteen orchestral works ; two hundred songs.

MEDTNER, NICHOLAS (1880–1951). Of German parentage, he trained in Moscow, and settled in England. Pianist. He composed much piano music, including two concertos.

MENDELSSOHN, FELIX (1809–1847) Of wealthy German–Jewish parentage. A young friend of Goethe. At fifteen had already written many symphonies. At seventeen wrote overture to *A Midsummer Night's Dream*. His music is always polished and perfected, and is of the less expansive, romantic type. *Works include :* overtures, *Fingal's Cave* ; oratorios, *Elijah* ; piano music, *Songs without Words* ; symphonies, a violin concerto and miscellaneous instrumental works.

MEYERBEER, GIACOMO (1791–1864). Of a wealthy German–Jewish family. A writer of operas, first in Italy, then in France. His style is loud and vigorous, and his work was criticised on the former count by Schumann. *Works include :* operas, *Robert le Diable, Les Huguenots, L'Africaine* ; ballet music ; oratorios and other church music, etc.

MILHAUD, DARIUS (1892–). A French " modernist " composer, working on polytonal lines. Has collaborated with the mystical poet Claudel, and has produced miscellaneous orchestral and church works.

MOEREN, ERNEST (1894–1950). Was born near London of Irish descent. He settled in Norfolk, where he composed various works, all showing strong folk-tune influence.

MONTEVERDI, CLAUDIO (1567–1643). Born at Cremona, Italy. Exponent of a freer and richer style in music ; he is of great importance in the history of musical development, in particular of opera. *Works include :* operas, *Orfeo, The Coronation of Poppaea* ; religious works ; twenty-one canzonettes, and numerous books of madrigals.

MORLEY, THOMAS (1557–1603). Elizabethan composer of instrumental and church music, and of madrigals. Organist of St. Paul's Cathedral and Gentleman of the Chapel Royal. Composed songs for some of Shakespeare's plays. He wrote a *Plaine and Easie Introduction to Practicall Music* (1597).

MOZART, WOLFGANG AMADEUS (1756–1791). Born in Salzburg. Began to give performances with his sister at the age of six. Composed the most " pure " instrumental music that has ever been written ; a "classical" composer in the strictest sense, and a most perfectly equipped musician. *Works include :* operas, nearly twenty, including *Figaro, Don Giovanni, The Magic Flute* ; symphonies, nearly fifty, including *The Jupiter, The Lintz* ; over twenty piano concertos ; twenty-seven string quartets ; forty violin sonatas ; etc.

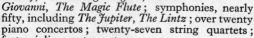

MURRILL, HERBERT (1909–52). Born in London. Professor at the Royal Academy of Music. Engaged in broadcasting work. Composed miscellaneous works, including one opera, *Man in Cage.*

MUSSORGSKY, MODESTE (1839–1881). A Russian composer who got much of his inspiration from folk tunes. His characteristic style is musical realism. His operas *Boris Godunof* and *Khovantchina* are his greatest works. He was one of the " Five " (see Borodin).

NICOLAI, KARL OTTO (1810–1849). Born in Konigsberg. Composer of operas, the most well-known being *The Merry Wives of Windsor.*

OFFENBACH, JAKOB (1819–1880). Born at Offenbach in Germany, which name he adopted as his own. He settled in Paris in early youth.

Composed light, melodious operettas of great popularity. *Works include : Orpheus in the Underworld ; Tales of Hoffmann.*

PALESTRINA, GIOVANNI PIERLUIGI DA (1525–1594). Born at Palestrina in Italy. One of the greatest composers of contrapuntal music for unaccompanied voices.

PALMGREN, SELIM (1878–1951). Finnish composer and pianist who favoured the smaller forms of instrumental music. Influenced by native folk tunes. Was chairman of the Sibelius Foundation, Helsinki. *Works include:* opera, *Daniel Hjort ;* two piano concertos ; piano music, etc.

PARRY, SIR HUBERT (1848–1918). Born in Bournemouth. Director of Royal College of Music. Professor of Music, Oxford. Prolific composer of choral-orchestral works of a very English type. Not so successful in purely instrumental music. *Works include : Blest Pair of Sirens ;* Blake's *Jerusalem ; Job ;* unaccompanied motets. Important literary works are *The Evolution of the Art of Music* and *Style in Musical Art.*

PIJPER, WILLEM (1894–1947). Born near Utrecht. He became music critic of a Utrecht newspaper. Composed miscellaneous works, later works being in an " atonal " idiom (see page 188).

POULENC, FRANCIS (1899–1963). Born in Paris. He became strongly opposed to the "romantic" element in music. *Works include :* ballet music, *Les biches, Les animaux modeles ;* two comic-operas ; cantata, *Le bal masqué ; Concert champêtre* for harpsichord and orchestra, much piano music, as well as orchestral and chamber works.

PROKOFIEV, SERGE (1891–1953). Was born in Russia, and travelled widely. His work is often classical in form, but the conception is "modernistic". Satire and realism are characteristic. *Works include:* operas, *Love for Three Oranges, The Flaming Angel,* etc.; ballets, *The Buffoon, L'Enfant prodigue,* etc.; orchestral music, *The Classical Symphony,* and four others; miscellaneous instrumental works.

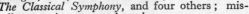

PUCCINI, GIACOMO (1858–1924). Born at Lucca of an Italian musical family. Composer of operas, melodious, flowing and typically Italian in style. Not highly original, but original enough to catch the public ear, hence his popularity. *Works include: Manon Lescaut; La Bohême; Tosca; Madame Butterfly; The Girl of the Golden West; Turandot,* etc.

PURCELL, HENRY (1659–1695). Born, probably, in Westminster. The greatest British composer of his age. Organist of the Chapel Royal, and in consequence produced much church music. *Works include:* opera, *Dido and Aeneas;* semi-operas, *Fairy Queen, King Arthur,* etc.; odes, songs and instrumental pieces.

QUILTER, ROGER (1877–1953). Born in Brighton. Composer of songs and incidental music for plays. *Children's Overture* (1920).

RACHMANINOV, SERGE (1873–1943). Born in Russia, died in California. Toured the world as a pianist. Composed a large number of works, including piano concertos, symphonies, operas, songs and piano solos.

RAMEAU, JEAN (1683–1764). Son of the organist of Dijon Cathedral. Toured Italy, then joined a troupe of wandering French actors. His writings on musical theory laid the foundation for modern study. Later received a Court appointment from Louis XIV. Has greatly influenced French music. *Works include :* twenty-four operas ; harpsichord pieces, etc.

RAVEL, MAURICE (1875–1937). Born near St. Jean de Luz, France. Like Debussy, of the " impressionist " school, but music is sharper, less fluid. Introduces technical innovations. *Work includes :* opera-ballet, *L'Enfant et les sortileges* ; ballets, *Daphnis et Chloe*, etc. ; orchestral works, *Bolero*, *Rapsodie espagnole* ; numerous instrumental and piano music ; *Pavane for a Dead Infanta*.

RAWSTHORNE, ALAN (1905–71). Born in Lancashire. Trained at Manchester College of Music. Has composed numerous works, including *Violin Concerto* (1948).

RIMSKY-KORSAKOF (1844–1908). A Russian Naval Officer who became Professor of Composition at Conservatory of St. Petersburg. His music is of great dramatic power with rhythmic force and orchestral colour (see Berlioz), strongly influenced by folk tunes. *Works include : Ivan the Terrible* ; *The Snow Maiden* ; *The Golden Cockerel*, etc. ; symphonic poem, *Sadko* ; three symphonies, and smaller works.

ROSSINI, GIOACCHINO (1792–1868). Born in Italy. At the age of thirty-seven he had written thirty-six operas, for the remaining forty years of his life he wrote none. Had a strong melodious sense—and humour, and the ability to combine instruments and voices. *Works include : The Barber of Seville, Otello, William Tell*, etc. ; *Stabat Mater* ; fifteen cantatas.

RUBBRA, EDMUND (1901–). Born in Northampton. Studied at Royal College of Music under Holst, Vaughan Williams and R. O. Morris. Lecturer, Music Faculty, Oxford University, 1947. Numerous compositions, five symphonies, piano concertos, choral works, etc.

SAINT-SAENS, CAMILLE (1835–1921). Of an old Norman family, he was for twenty years organist of the Madeleine, Paris. Composed with facility. Wrote the first French symphonic poem (*Omphale's Spinning Wheel*). *Works include :* operas, *Samson and Delilah, Helène* ; ballet and incidental music ; four symphonic poems ; piano and violin concertos.

SCARLATTI, A. (1660–1725). Born in Sicily. His development of harmony and form prepared the ground for Haydn, greatest works being his operas and chamber cantatas. *Works include :* five hundred chamber cantatas; two hundred masses.

SCARLATTI, D. (1685–1757) Son of the above. Great keyboard performer. Composed over six hundred harpsichord sonatas, and keyboard technique owes much to him.

SCHOËNBERG, ARNOLD (1874–1951). Born in Vienna of Jewish parents. Early works show influence of Wagner. In his later works he developed original harmonic system through which to express German romanticism. Used the twelve-note scale (see page 188). Professor of Music, University of California, 1936–44. *Works include :* operas; drama with music; song cycle, *Das Buch der hängenden Garten*; *Pierrot Lunaire*, for speech-song and chamber orchestra, etc.

SCHUBERT, FRANZ (1797–1828). Died at the early age of thirty-one. He lived in Vienna at the same time as Beethoven, and like him, belongs both to the classical school of Mozart, and to the beginnings of the romantic movement. He had a gift for pure melody, especially for the solo song which has so greatly added to his fame. *Works include :* operas and operettas; choral and religious works; nine symphonies; piano sonatas, etc.; six hundred and six songs, including seventy-one settings of Goethe, forty-two of Schiller.

SCHUMANN, ROBERT (1810–1856). Born in Saxony. Composer of the less exuberant type of romantic music. His wife, Clara, a fine pianist, popularized his music after his early death due to a mental disorder. *Works include :* four symphonies ; five concert overtures ; songs and piano pieces, etc.

SHOSTAKOVITCH, DIMITRI (1906–). A bolshevist composer, who believes music must have a political basis. *Works include :* symphonies, *The " October " Symphony, The May Day Symphony* ; operas.

SIBELIUS, JEAN (1865–1957). Born in Finland. At thirty-two received a Government grant to enable him to devote himself to composition. Music shows national feeling, and the bleak winters and short, bright summers of his native country are given musical expression in his work. His later compositions are individualistic and uncompromising. *Works include :* seven symphonies ; tone-poems, *Karelia,* four legends, *Swan of Tuonela, Finlandia* ; incidental music to *The Tempest,* etc.

SKRIABIN, ALEXANDER (1872–1915). Russian composer, originally an Army officer. Best known for his piano music ; wrote also three symphonies and lesser instrumental works. He tried to express his strange mystical and philosophical theories in large orchestral works such as *The Divine Poem.*

SMETANA, BEDRICH (1824–1884). A national and nationalist Czech composer, much honoured in his own country. His operas are Czech in musical idiom and in their material. An advocate of the symphonic poem, four of his own being composed when he was deaf. Died in an asylum. *Works include :* operas, *The Bartered Bride, Two Widows,* etc. ; symphonic poems, *Wallenstein's Camp* ; cycle, *My Country,* etc. ; Czech dances and songs.

SMYTH, ETHEL (1858–1944). Born in London, daughter of an artillery general. Made a Dame in 1922. Studied in Germany. A suffragette. *Works include :* operas, *The Forest, The Wreckers, The Boatswain's Mate, Fête Galante* ; also orchestral music.

STANFORD, CHARLES V. (1852–1924). Born in Dublin. Professor of Composition, Royal College of Music, and Professor of Music at Cambridge University. Conductor of Bach Choir (1885–1892). Composed seven operas, seven symphonies, etc. ; edited collection of Irish songs.

STRAUSS FAMILY, THE, were the chief promoters of the Viennese Waltz. Johann II's waltzes (1825–1899) are those chiefly remembered today.

STRAUSS, RICHARD (1864–1949). Born in Munich of a musical family (no relation to the above) ; the most successful of Wagner's successors. His orchestration is brilliant. Outstanding are his symphonic poems, which are of a passionate, emotional nature, sometimes excessively so.

Works include: operas, *Der Rosenkavalier*, *Salome*, etc.; symphonic poems, *Till Eulenspiegel*; ballet and instrumental music.

STRAVINSKY, IGOR (1882–1970). Born of Russian parents. He decided, through the persuasion of Rimsky-Korsakof, to devote himself to music. Studied in Paris and composed music for Diaghilef's Russian Ballet. Experienced opposition when he ignored conventional harmony and form (e.g. *Rite of Spring*). Later he adopted neo-classical style, and abandoned his earlier Russian characteristics. *Works include:* ballets, *The Fire Bird*, *Petrushka*, *The Rite of Spring*, *The Nightingale*; symphonies, *Symphonies of Wind Instruments in Memory of Debussy*; orchestral works.

SULLIVAN, Sir A. (1842–1900). Born in London. He wrote numerous works, but his fame chiefly rests on light operas written in collaboration with Gilbert. Had sense of melody, and of fun, and a lightness of touch. *Works include: Trial by Jury, H.M.S. Pinafore, The Pirates of Penzance, Patience, Iolanthe, Mikado, The Yeomen of the Guard*, etc.

SUPPÉ, FRANZ VON (1819–1895). Born in Dalmatia. He wrote over one hundred and fifty operas and operettas. Overtures include *Poet and Peasant* and *Light Cavalry*.

TALLIS, THOMAS (bet. 1505 and 1510–1585). An Elizabethan composer. Joint organist, with Byrd, of the Chapel Royal. Harmonized the plainsong Responses of the Anglican Service as arranged by Merbecke, which are still constantly used. He wrote much church music and some keyboard and string music.

TCHAIKOVSKY, PETER (1840–1893). A Russian composer who came under the influence of Balakiref and Rimsky-Korsakof. Unlike most of his Russian contemporaries, never sought to adapt folk material. His music is strongly emotional, his life unusual. *Works include :* ten operas, *The Queen of Spades,* etc.; six symphonies; symphonic poems; lesser works and ballet music. *Swan Lake, Sleeping Princess, Casse-noisette.*

TELEMANN, GEORGE (1681–1767). Born in Magdeburg, Germany. Highly regarded in his day. *Works include* over forty settings of the Passion, and forty operas. Much of his chamber music is being revived today.

TIPPETT, MICHAEL (1905–). Born in London, studied at the Royal College of Music. Was formerly Director of Morley College. Has made important contributions to the field of orchestra. *Works include :* Symphony in B♭; Concerto for Double String Orchestra; *Fantasia on a theme of Handel;* chamber music; oratorio, *A Child of Our Time;* piano music.

VAUGHAN WILLIAMS, RALPH (1872–1958). Born in Gloucestershire. Studied at the Royal College of Music. Also studied with Max Bruch in Berlin. Work individual and of increasing power, allows no musical convention to stand in the way of expressive treatment. Interested in folk- and Tudor music. *Works include :* six symphonies,

The Sea Symphony (1910), *The London Symphony* (1920), *The Pastoral* (1922), etc. ; *The E. Minor* (1948), *Sinfonia Antarctica* (1953) ; choral orchestral works ; songs, *Linden Lea* ; operas, *Hugh the Drover*, *Sir John in Love* ; ballets *Job* ; etc.

VERDI, GIUSEPPE (1813–1901). The greatest Italian opera composer of the 19th century. Early period is melodramatic (*Rigoletto*), later developed a more dignified tone (*Aida*). When he was seventy-four, wrote *Otello*, to be followed by *Falstaff*. Had a gift for melody, to which he gradually added finer orchestration and richer depth. *Works include : Il Trovatore, La Traviata, Rigoletto, Aida, Otello, etc. ; also Requiem ; Stabat Mater.*

VIVALDI, ANTONIO (1675?–1741). Born probably in Venice, died in Vienna. Especially important as a composer of concertos of which he wrote nearly four hundred ; and choral works.

WAGNER, RICHARD (1813–1883). One of the most bold and energetic of composers. Born in Leipzig of a theatrical family. In him the dramatic side of the German romantic movement finds its fullest expression. In order to achieve flexibility and characterization in his operas, he used the *Leitmotiv* (see page 135). He wrote his own libretti, and staged his own operas. He built a theatre at Bayreuth under patronage of the King of Bavaria, where his works could be performed under ideal conditions. *Works include : The Flying Dutchman, Tannhäuser, Lohengrin, The Ring, Tristan and Isolde, The Mastersingers, Parsifal.*

WALTON, WILLIAM (1902–). Born at Oldham. Composes sparingly, but work is of high quality, including concertos, an oratorio, *Belshazzar's Feast,* and one symphony (1935). Hon. Doctor of Music, Durham 1937, Oxford 1942.

WARLOCK, PETER (1894–1930). Real name Philip Heseltine. Under his own name edited Elizabethan lute-songs, and wrote on Delius, etc. Under "Peter Warlock" composed chamber works and songs. Died in London at thirty-six, it is thought by his own hand.

WEBER, CARL MARIA VON (1786–1826). Born in Lubeck. Founder of national, romantic German opera. Died in London, where he had come on invitation of Kemble to conduct *Oberon* at Covent Garden. *Works include :* operas, *Der Freischütz, Euryanthe, Oberon* ; piano music, etc.

WEBERN, ANTON VON (1883–1945). Born in Vienna. A follower of Schoënberg. Composed delicate works, on a small scale.

WEELKES, THOMAS (1575 ?–1623). Organist of Chichester Cathedral, and composer of organ music and madrigals, including the famous madrigal : *As Vesta was from Latmos hill descending.* He contributed to the " *Triumphs of Oriana* ", a collection of madrigals in praise of Queen Elizabeth Tudor.

WILBYE, JOHN (1574–1638). Born at Diss, in Norfolk. Served the Kytson family, of Bury St. Edmunds, all his life. Considered the greatest composer of madrigals (*Adieu Sweet Amaryllis,* etc.).

WOLF, HUGO (1860–1903). By some considered second only to Schubert as a song-writer. After being dismissed from the Vienna Conservatory, he settled for four years in a small village near Vienna, where he wrote feverishly, one song after another. He died, in an asylum, at the age of forty-three. He also wrote some instrumental pieces and an opera.

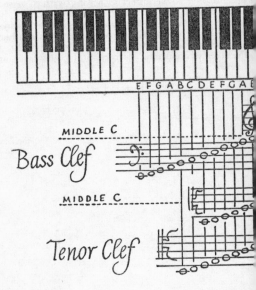

PLAN OF PIANOFORTE
RELATIVE POSITIONS O

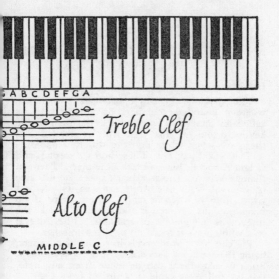

Treble Clef

Alto Clef

MIDDLE C

BOARD SHOWING THE
FS IN COMMON USE

AN EXPLANATION OF SOME TERMS USED WITHIN THE TEXT

INTERVALS

The distance in pitch between two notes, whether sounded together, or successively, is called an interval. On studying the plan of the keyboard on pp. 184–5, it will be noticed that there are seven white notes of different names— A, B, C, D, E, F, G. These notes, except B and C and E and F, have a black note placed between them. Where there is a black note, the distance or interval from one white note to its adjacent white note is a *whole tone*. Where there is no black note, as between B and C and E and F, the interval is a *half-tone* or *semitone*. The interval of a whole tone is made up of two semitones.

We can refer to intervals in terms of numbers, using the semitone as a standard of measurement. Such measurement can be made from any note, but the following table is compiled from C:

From C to D there are 2 semitones, the interval is a Major 2nd.

From C to E there are 4 semitones, the interval is a Major 3rd.

From C to F there are 5 semitones, the interval is a Perfect 4th.

From C to G there are 7 semitones, the interval is a Perfect 5th.

From C to A there are 9 semitones, the interval is a Major 6th.

From C to B there are 11 semitones, the interval is a Major 7th.

From C to C there are 12 semitones, the interval is a Perfect 8th (octave).

Certain intervals have been omitted, namely those from C to each of the black notes (those with 3, 6, 8 and 10 semitones). The black notes are named according to their relationship to their adjacent white notes. Thus the black note between C and D can be considered as C raised by half a tone (C sharp (♯)) or D lowered by half a tone (D flat (♭)). Similarly, the black note between D and E can be called either D♯ (D sharp) or E♭ (E flat), and so on:

From C to D♭ there is 1 semitone, the interval is a Minor 2nd.

From C to E♭ there are 3 semitones, the interval is a Minor 3rd.

From C to F♯ there are 6 semitones, the interval is an Augmented 4th.

From C to G♭ there are 6 semitones, the interval is a Diminished 5th.

From C to A♭ there are 8 semitones, the interval is a Minor 6th.

From C to B♭ there are 10 semitones, the interval is a Minor 7th.

When an interval is greater than an octave it is said to be compound:

From C to D (above the octave) is 9th.

From C to E (above the octave) is 10th.

From C to F (above the octave) is 11th.

From C to G (above the octave) is 12th.

From C to A (above the octave) is 13th, etc.

SCALES

On playing the white notes from C to C we shall find we are playing what is known as the Scale of C major—" C " because it begins on C; "major" because the interval from C to E is a major 3rd. It is known as *diatonic* because there are both tones and semitones in it.

On playing the same series of notes, but substituting E♭ for E natural, we shall find we are playing the scale of C minor—" minor " because the interval from C to E♭ is a minor 3rd (minor = less; major = greater). This scale is also known as *diatonic*, because it has both tones and semitones.

If all the white and black notes are played in succession: C, D♭, D, E♭, E, etc., there will be a semitone between every note. This form of scale is called *chromatic*.

Other rarer forms of scales are the *whole tone scale*, which, built from C, would consist of C, D, E, F♯, G♯, A♯, and the *Pentatonic* (five note) scale, similar to the major scale, without its 4th and 7th notes—it can be found by playing the black notes only, beginning on F♯.

Atonal music : Music not composed in any definite key; twelve-note music is atonal.

Polytonal music : A 20th-century device of composition in which music may be written in several different keys at once.

Twelve-note music : A modern system of composition used by Schoënberg and his followers, employing the twelve notes of the chromatic scale, and giving equal importance to every note. For instance, a theme must contain all twelve notes, each appearing once, but any rhythm may be used. The same notes may be grouped vertically to form chords.

INDEX OF MUSICAL INSTRUMENTS

189

Printed in Great Britain by Richard Clay (The Chaucer Press), Ltd.,
Bungay, Suffolk
1481.574